Language of Life

answers to modern crises
in an ancient way of
speaking

Language of Life

answers to modern crises in an ancient way of speaking

Milt Markewitz
&
Ruth L. Miller

With contributions by Batya Podos

Language of Life: answers to modern crises in an ancient way of speaking

© 2013 Milt Markewitz & Ruth L. Miller

Contributor: Batya Podos
Cover Art: Ken Roffmann

Portal Center Press
Gleneden Beach, Oregon 97388

www.portalcenterpress.com

for more information about this book and related topics, go to the website: www.natureslanguage.com

ISBN: 978-1-936902-11-8
Spirituality • Social Sciences

Printed in the U.S.A.

We are faced with a whole series of global problems which are harming the biosphere and human life in alarming ways that may soon become irreversible....

Ultimately, these problems must be seen as just different facets of one single crisis, which is largely a crisis of perception. It derives from the fact that most of us, and especially our large social institutions, subscribe to the concepts of an outdated worldview, a perception of reality inadequate for dealing with our overpopulated, globally interconnected world... ~ Fritjof Capra, *The Web of Life*

Dedication

By Milt—

My late friend, Ken Roffmann, gave me a copy of *The Cipher of Genesis* over a decade ago, and I subsequently gave a copy to the late Rabbi Aryeh Hirschfield. When Aryeh told me that he would be using a learning from the book in a class he was teaching at Trinity Episcopal Church here in Portland, I asked him if he'd be willing to facilitate a book group. We agreed on a day, time, and frequency, and we subsequently met almost every 3 weeks for over 2 years. Ken was living in Salt Lake City when we began, but joined our group for the last year of study when he moved back to Portland. He was the 'resident expert' and quickly became fast friends with Aryeh.

Sadly but poignantly, my last conversation with Aryeh in 2008 was a couple days before he left for his son's wedding in Mexico where he tragically passed away in a drowning accident. The last thing we talked about was my fascination and interpretation of Suares' 3x9 matrix, and he said that further understanding, perhaps joint teaching, would be our work when he returned.

The last time I was with Ken was a couple days before I left for the Parliament of World Religions in Melbourne, Australia, in the fall of 2009. We co-facilitated a "Cipher of Genesis" workshop in which Ken was, although in the last stages of life with leukemia, his fully energetic, brilliant self.

I dedicate this book to these two mentors and dear friends.

Contents

Foreword	i
PART 1 PATTERNS & WORLDS	1
Introduction	3
Hebrew, Sanskrit, and English	7
Prima Lingua	8
Alternative Language Structures	11
Spoken and Written Language	12
Hebrew as a Living Language	21
Emergent Patterns derived from Suares' Work	25
Three Worlds	31
PART 2 STORIES	35
The Binding of Isaac	37
Creation	45
A Creation Story	48
In the Wilderness	53
Batya's Interpretation of Yitro and his Role	54
Milt's Perspective on Yitro	63
"Hidden" Patterns & Possibilities	65
PART 3 LIFE	73
The Story We Live	75
Changing the Story	78
Wisdom Consciousness	85
Honoring Differences	93
The Power of the Human Dynamics Model	93
Understanding Transformation through Ceremony	97
The Indigenous Way of Thinking	103
Three Major Paradigm Shifts	108
Understanding Systems	111
Living Systems: The Theory Underlying Sustainability	119
A Living Systems Curriculum	122
Teaching the Curriculum	125

Applying the Theory	125
The Living Systems Experience	128
Hope	131
Appreciative Inquiry, Ecological Harmony	137
The Fairview A-I Process	139
Transformation & Transcendence	145
Grace & Gratitude	147
The Power of Gratitude	147
Speaking a Language of Life	151
Listening to Indigenous Voices	151
Living Language, Sustainable Life	157
Finding Answers	158
Gratitudes	161

Foreword

> There are two fundamentally different sources of cognition. One is the application of existing frameworks (downloading) and the other accessing one's inner knowing. All true innovation in science, business, and society is based on the latter... ~ *Brian Arthur*[1]

—*Milt Markewitz*

From time to time we learn something so seminal that we feel we are experiencing a basic truth—it clarifies questions we hold about life, informs our way of thinking and being, and provides a framework for more profound learning. One particular jewel, a 3x9 matrix of the ancient Hebrew language, is found in Carlos Suares' inspiring book, *The Cipher of Genesis: The Original Code of the Qabala as Applied to the Scriptures*. It's described in detail in the chapter on Hebrew Language later in this book. Several other jewels from his book are also included in these writings.

Suares combines the 22 basic Hebrew characters plus the 5 characters that are called "final" or *sofit*, that appear differently when they are at the end of a word, forming a 27-character system of letter-numbers that he then articulates in a 3x9 matrix. The 3 rows of his matrix represent three of the 4 Worlds in the Qabala (the Jewish mystical tradition, based on the idea that we are constantly developing and evolving), which for me represent three realities—Archetypal, Existential, and Cosmological—each with an apparently different scientific basis. The 9 columns appear to be perhaps all that is necessary and sufficient to support all life processes. The matrix leads one to explore a whole new range of patterns to be found in Ancient Hebrew.

Now I'm not your typical Hebrew scholar. My early education almost all centered around math and Newtonian physics, with only a couple classes in quantum physics, and my problem-

---

[1] Brian Arthur, Santa Fe Institute, in conversation with Otto Scharmer as reported in the Executive Summary of *Theory U*, p.5

solving career with IBM used primarily mechanistic approaches for every type of problem. The exception came when I worked with people from other cultures; then I realized that they sometimes discerned organizations and manufacturing processes as living systems rather than machines.

After I retired from IBM a friend asked me to help him with a sustainability-oriented start-up company, in order to do which we were going to have to better understand the consciousness of all life. Once we had seed money and a prototype, I left the company in good hands and went back to graduate school for a Masters degree in 'Whole System Design' in which the curriculum was primarily based on Living Systems. My graduation project was to see if I could get a small town in Oregon to define their desired future based on several facets of being sustainable, and in the process, persuade their public schools to develop the curricula necessary for both education in the schools and building a 'learning community.' My advisor, the late Dr. Elaine Jessen, insisted that I do a theory paper on my project. What became clear was that the theory that underlies sustainability is Living Systems Theory. Also, as part of my class work, I was on a Design Team to teach Living Systems to my cohort with Dr. Fritjof Capra. From that work I developed a Living Systems curriculum that I now teach whenever I'm asked. A significant part of that teaching is trying to understand how Living Systems organize themselves. A key portion of that understanding is recognizing what is both necessary and sufficient to support life.

It's not too surprising, then, that when I encountered Suares' work, based as it is on what appeared to be the processes necessary and sufficient to support life, I saw a model of Living Systems.

I felt some confirmation of my discernment of Saures' work a couple years ago when I attended an interfaith service in which Arun Gandhi was the guest speaker. He spoke about going to his grandfather, Mahatma Gandhi, and asking him to explain peace. His grandfather gave him a kernel of grain that Arun subsequently put in a box. When he looked in the box days later, the kernel had shriveled up. With the shriveled kernel in hand, he once again asked his grandfather to explain peace. Now his grandfather explained that if he had planted the kernel in soil and nurtured it with water, he would have a plant that created its own seeds, and, if he desired, after a relatively short time and some diligence he could have a whole field of grain.

I thought this to be a rather abstract understanding of peace until I thought of Shalom, the Hebrew word for peace.

I was introduced to Arun after the service and asked him if his father was energetically connected to Sanskrit. With a look of surprise he answered 'yes, how did you know?' I told him of my study of ancient Hebrew, and the interpretation I had come to for the Hebrew word for peace, *Shalom*. It's made up of four characters: *Sheen, Lammed, Vav,* and a *final Mem (sofit)*. The Cosmic Breath of G*d is represented by the letter *Sheen*, and the Cosmic Perfect seed is the *final Mem*, from which the Archetypal life process of fertilization, *(Vav)* is created, and from this fertilization emerges Existential Organic life, *Lammed*.

The story that Mahatma Gandhi told his grandson, Arun, seems to me to be the same story told by this single collection of ancient Hebrew characters that we now think of as the word *Shalom*.

In that moment I was struck by the possibility that every combination of letters that we read as a word, is in fact a story, and that possibly the ancient writings are most accurately understood when each word is understood as a story.

With that idea in mind, I asked my friend, mentor, and colleague, Ms. Batya Podos, who is an incredible storyteller, if she'd like to work with me on this book. When I told her of my encounter with Arun Gandhi, and how his whole story about peace was imbedded in our word for peace, 'Shalom', she was very excited. I asked her if she'd like to apply this sort of understanding to the words at the opening of Genesis, the first day of creation, and possibly subsequent days; as well as the Exodus experience in the desert as it related to Moses' relationship with his father-in-law Yitro; and my interpretation of the 'Binding of Isaac'. She responded with an enthusiastic, 'Yes', and her work is included later in this book. Thank you Batya, for all your hard work and added value.

Dr. Ruth Miller and I have been friends for years, with our paths crossing over and over again as we were drawn by our common interests in Systems Science, Education, and particularly Learning Organizations, plus mysticism, spirituality, the new sciences and interfaith work. At one point years ago I sublet an office from Ruth and we did some teaching and writing together. Last year I invited her to present her work comparing modern religious and spiritual writings with ancient texts to the Interfaith Council of Greater Portland. As we were leaving, I suggested that perhaps there was another book waiting to be written, based on a book by Carlo Suares, *The Cipher of Genesis: The Original Code of the Qabala as Applied to the Scriptures*, and how it informs us about both the ancient texts and our current crisis of living unsustainably. We made a date for lunch, where I shared my current understandings and writings, and Ruth told me of her work with Sankskrit terms that outlined a similar model. Then she, in her brilliant way, outlined this book right there as we talked.

And so we three have proceeded to contribute, from rather different perspectives, to this integration of ancient wisdom with modern understandings. Our hope is to stimulate deeper study and conversations and that, through the process, people will find ways in which enlightened use of language can contribute to finding balance, harmony, and peace in the World.

A Note from Ruth:

Milt is an amazing man who has followed his passion for decades. Each time our paths have crossed it's been because he was ready to deepen his understanding and explore a new approach—and through our dialogs we've both always come away with both. Now, our paths have brought us to this attempt to comprehend the essential message hidden within the language of Hebrew, and to relate it to the comparable messages expressed in other times and places, in the hope of bringing our world closer to a sustainable way of living. Doing so has been an adventure in itself, deepening our understandings of concepts and teachings we've been working with for years. We hope it will do the same for you.

PART 1

PATTERNS & WORLDS

"If the doors of perception were cleansed every thing would appear to man as it is, Infinite. For man has closed himself up, till he sees all things thro' narrow chinks of his cavern."

~ William Blake

Introduction

"The greatest revolution of our time is in the way we see the world. The mechanistic paradigm underlying the Industrial Growth Society gives way to the realization that we belong to a living, self-organizing cosmos.... This realization changes everything. It changes our perceptions of who we are and what we need, and how we can trustfully act together for a decent, noble future." ~ *Joanna Macy* [2]

Milt Markewitz

My current life work is largely driven by the quest to make our Earth ecologically sustainable for all future generations, with the belief that all other facets of sustainability will follow. The graphic on the following page, derived from work of Joanna Macy, helps me in that it serves as a framework for both achieving sustainability, and for understanding how we have institutionalized not being sustainable.

It isn't that there's not a profusion of very good, well intentioned people, doing some extraordinary work. Still, as necessary as it is to recycle, reuse, grow gardens, spend time with Nature, conserve energy, refocus technology, etc., it isn't enough. Furthermore, we're compounding the situation with the belief that doing just what we're doing is enough and having the hubris to accept a leadership mantel for teaching others the solution to our dilemma.

Macy names what we are currently doing as 'Holding Actions', and, while they're essential for incrementally raising consciousness, they're inadequate for achieving sustainability. The graphic shows that the bridge between 'Holding Actions' and the higher consciousness necessary for sustainability, the 'Paradigm Shifts,' is 'Systemic Understanding'.

This concept, "Systemic Understanding," underlies much of what is being said in this book, so it's worth taking a moment to

---

[2] www.joannamacy.net

look at it. It's based on a set of ideas that grew out of biology and have been applied to everything from disease management to ecology to computer science and space travel. The fundamental concept is that any functioning unit has elements working together to accomplish something, and it's the relationships between those elements that govern the whole. The problem is that the mechanical view of systems has taken over.

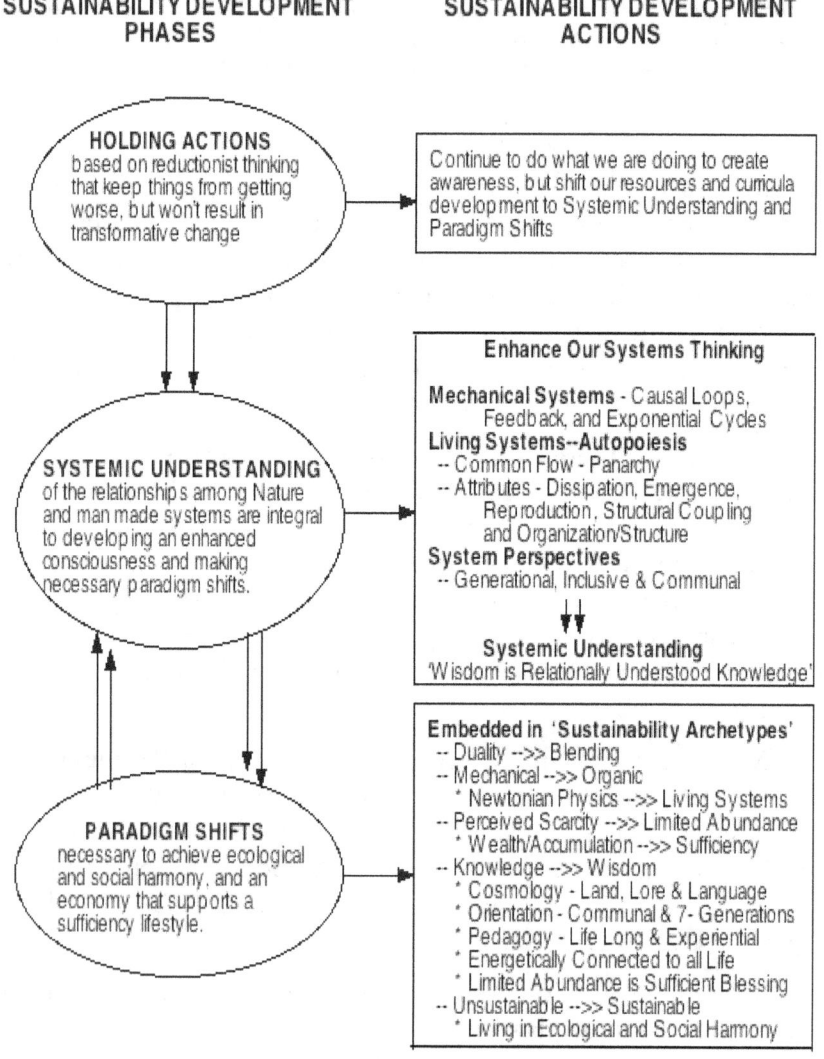

The 3 approaches to Systems Thinking (shown in the middle right hand box of the graphic) that need to be further developed are:

- Making the shift from Mechanical Causal Loops to an Organic energies and flows;
- Formalizing our understanding of Living Systems; and
- Recognizing that there are widely different system perspectives that must be blended to achieve a comprehensive systemic understanding.

Paradigm Shifts will be framed in terms of 'Archetypes for Sustainability', and the importance of language in shaping how we perceive life, connect with the natural world, flow with change, and live each day in accordance with this world-view.

The essence for all of this is derived from one very small portion of Carlos Suares', *The Cipher of Genesis: The Original Code of the Qabala as Applied to the Scriptures*, a 3x9 matrix of the 27 Hebrew 'letter-numbers'. Suares explains that the 3 rows as represent three worlds—Archetypal, Existential, and Cosmological--in which we all exist. From this I assumed that the Cosmological letter-numbers should drive the stories of Genesis, and proceeded to analyze "The Binding of Isaac" from this perspective. What emerged was a very different story. It wasn't about G*d asking Avraham to sacrifice his son, but of revelation and the creation of the Jewish 'DNA' that would be carried in all the descendents of Isaac.

What I then discovered, primarily through working with Batya, is how deeply I've internalized the 9 columns into my understanding of Living Systems, and how integral this is to all of my emergent understandings and writing. It is also integral to them in the much broader sense that if we cannot discern all our systems—social, business, non-profit, educational, religious, etc.—as alive, supplemented with mechanical systems, then each of these systems institutionalizes to one degree or another our non-sustainable ways.

Finally, it has become clear that, if this vitality is imbedded in our language, then we develop an intuitive understanding. If it is not, then we probably need to develop educational bridges to these ways of learning and knowing. This is a primary 'Paradigm Shift' that is critical to the survival of our specie.

Greg Braden explains in the Foreword to *The Cipher of Genesis* that the essence of Suares' book, is that for today's scholars who search for meaning and 'truth' from the ancient texts, "their monumental task will not lead them any nearer the Source, not only because the Bible is untranslatable but, strange as it may seem, because it is already hopelessly translated in Hebrew."

From this it seems as if the only chance we have to ever know what the ancient writings really convey is to understand and utilize the ancient languages as they were spoken and understood several thousand years ago. But perhaps there are ways that we can know at least much more than we know today and unhook from the misleading beliefs we've developed over the millennia.

What follows is an attempt to build bridges back to an understanding of being in harmony in all facets of our lives by internalizing Suares' teachings of the Ancient Hebrew, listening to the cultures who never lost their ancient language, and suggesting other learning to help us shift our non-life-affirming Western ways.

The remainder of this book will look at how language affects our experience of the stories we live by. Then we will explore and identify the 'Paradigm Shifts' necessary to move toward sustainability, and finally, offer some teachings to better understand the organic processes of all facets of our lives so that sustainable ways of being might flourish in our culture.

Hebrew, Sanskrit, and English

Ruth L. Miller

Having grown up in a family of anthropologists and art historians, some of whom were Christian, some of whom were Jewish, and some of whom had lived in India, I've had a fascination with languages and their relationships all my life. I still remember my delight when Grandmother told me *pajama* was a Hindi word, and the awe I felt when I realized that the Hebrew *Shalom*, the Arabic *Sala'am*, and the Hindi *Shanti-Om*, were all essentially the same word saying exactly the same thing. The interrelationships between languages became even clearer as I studied Latin and French, and picked up a little Spanish.

As I pursued a degree in anthropology the "Language and Culture" class was one of my favorites. There I saw that the language we learn as children must shape our thought processes for the rest of our lives—which idea, I found out, is the Whorf-Sapir hypothesis of language relativism. It turns out that many of the assumptions that English-speakers (and others whose language derives from Greek and Latin) have about the nature of the universe are, in fact, a product of the structure of our language, and may not have much to do with how the universe is structured, at all!

Time, for example, is experienced differently in cultures whose language doesn't include a past tense or a future tense. While we tend to focus on what has happened or will happen, people in other cultures may not even think about such things, being trained by the language they speak to see their experience as a continuous or cyclical unfolding. Or their idea of "on time" may be very different from ours.

As I studied cybernetics and systems in graduate school, I came to understand more fully how that worked and why the language we speak is so important. Communication is the means by which all systems are organized and managed, and the language used (whether a computer-programming language or a human language) limits the development options. So, it was clear that since human beings function as systems, both biologically and mentally, our developmental processes are defined in large part by the language we speak, read, write, and think in. And, as anthropologists and psychologists have discovered, this applies to the core values and assumptions that guide our decisions, as well as our current interactions.

When illness and my own healing process required that I examine more fully the spiritual teachings and core principles I lived by, I studied the Bible and other sacred texts in a new way. In the process, I discovered that the first writers of the New Testament were Greek, not Hebrew, and that even the Old Testament, the Hebrew Bible, had been translated into Latin and then into English from Greek, not Hebrew. Knowing what I knew about Latin and the translation process, I knew right away what that meant: there was very likely almost no similarity between what Jesus and the prophets had actually said and what I had been taught in church and temple. It was time to get clear about what I truly believed and where it came from—and what I learned was fascinating.

Prima Lingua

For nearly 2000 years, Western European scholars have learned 3 languages as essential to study the most important aspects of Western history. These were: Latin, the language of the Roman Republic and Empire; Greek, the language of the Athenian scholars and New Testament authors; and Hebrew, the language of the Old Testament, the Hebrew Bible. And, for most of those years, most of those scholars believed that Hebrew was the *prima lingua*, the language spoken by the very first human beings.

The idea that Hebrew was the oldest of human languages was firmly established by the early Christian bishop and scholar, Jerome, about 300 years after the New Testament was written. Using a Greek translation of the book of Genesis as his primary text, it was clear to him that God and Adam spoke to each other in Hebrew. From there he surmised that someone, most likely a man named Heber, had survived the Tower of Babel still able to speak his native tongue and passed it on to his descendents, including Abraham, and down to Jesus and his disciples.

This explanation created some dissonance among scholars for the next thousand years or so, for on the one hand they were taught to despise Jews for having crucified their Messiah, but on the other hand they sought the wisdom held by these speakers of the very language that Messiah spoke. So they went into the ghettos to learn what could not be taught in the church.

By the time of the European Enlightenment it was becoming clear that while Hebrew was indeed one of the oldest of languages, it was not, in fact, the oldest. Human beings had lived in other places than the children of Israel for many years before even Noah's ark was built. So, through the late 1800s, it became very popular for scholars studying antiquity to develop maps of the relationships between ancient cultures and their languages.

By the mid-1900s, it had been settled: Sumerian was the first written language, about 4000 years b.c.e. ("before the common era"), and the Sanskrit *Vedas* were probably the oldest written works still read and spoken. Egyptian hieroglyphs were more or less concurrent with Sumerian cuneiform, along with a "proto-Hebrew", with signs and symbols not too different from the formal Hebrew of Torah. Here's a typical chart relating them.

There were several other written languages developing during that same period, all around Asia and the Mediterranean, Chinese among them. Greek finally entered the picture about 600 b.c.e. and Latin took form about 200 b.c.e. The relatively young English (in its King James/Shakespearean form), along with modern French, Italian, and Spanish began to emerge over a thousand years later, in the 1500s. Until then, Latin was the common language across Europe and the Mediterranean.

Most of these languages derived from an even older one, used by people emerging out of the Caucasus and moving through what is now Iran, now called Aryan. It appears that waves of raiders would drive herds of cattle out of the Caucasus and across Asia every two hundred years or so, taking what they liked and destroying the farmlands of the villages they encountered.[3] Today their language is known as Indo-European, the root of virtually every language from the southern tip of India through the northern tip of Scotland, including English (Basque, Finnish, and Tamil being exceptions). And, if we read the oldest texts, whether in Sumerian or Sanskrit, we can learn a lot about both the language and the people who spoke, wrote, and lived it –and find many familiar root words.

Languages of Separation

From those texts it's clear: this is a language of conquest and takeover, of empire-building through destruction of indigenous communities, and of bragging about having done so. It's a language with many terms for various forms of weapons, and only one for an intimate, caring relationship. It has ways to describe

---

[3] I explain this process more fully in my book *Mary's Power, embracing the divine feminine as the age of invasion and empire ends.*

the past and the past before the past, and to describe the immediate future and the future beyond the future, and one for the present moment. It has lots of superlatives: "best" and "most" and "highest" and all kinds of other "-ests", and many ways to compare one thing against another. In it, a noun—a person, place, or thing—has priority over a process—a verb—and there are far more ways to do something to something than to be.

At the same time, it's a language in which it's possible to capture the minutiae of life and the expansiveness of the cosmos. It has scope and potential and possibility built into it—which may be largely responsible for the tremendous scientific advances that have occurred in the cultures that derive their languages from it.

It also evolves. We can see that in the plethora of languages that have emerged from it and in our modern experience: new words are made up and added into every Indo-European language all the time. As a result, few people who lived in the U.S. in the 1800s could understand most modern Americans—any more than most modern kids could understand the Shakespearean English of a few centuries before.[4]

Still, the basic structure remains—a subject acts on an object in the past, present, or future—and they are held separate: the actor, the action, and the object being acted upon.

Alternative Language Structures

By contrast, the Hopi, whose name means "people of peace," do not speak of past or future actions or states, but experience the constant unfolding of an always-existent developmental process—often referred to as the "Hopi Myth."

Hawaiian and most other Polynesian languages are constructed, not by combining verbs and nouns, but by connecting concepts and ideals and relating them to experience. The famous word *Aloha,* for example, is neither verb nor noun, but represents an integration of the realization that we need to stop and breathe

---

[4] In France this was occurring so rapidly that the government actually created an institute to monitor and limit "acceptable" changes to French.

to be aware of what's real and the idea of Infinite Spirit experienced as peace, love, happiness, and well-being.[5]

The Inuit language of the people most of us know as Eskimos has a huge set of descriptors for the environment. There are, for example, more words for the way snow falls and blows and drifts and changes than most English speakers can imagine possible.

The film *The Gods Must Be Crazy*, through humorous portrayals of encounters between Americans, Europeans, urban Africans and indigenous hunters from the Kalahari wilderness, illustrates how much difference there is between a culture with a language that includes a word that means "mine" and one that doesn't. And films like *Dancing with Wolves* and *The Last of the Dog Men* illustrate the attractiveness of such a sharing culture for someone whose life has been torn apart by a culture of violence based on perceived ownership. In such cultures there's no such problem because there's no such concept—and no such word.

In fact, many languages have incorporated English (or French or Spanish or Russian or German) words and phrases because they have no such concept in their own. To do business with us, or to work with tourists or as helpers, or to participate in our scientific research, they've had to adopt our language—which ultimately means they adopt aspects of our culture.

Spoken and Written Language

And it's not just the words that make a difference. The form of language—oral or written; alphabet-based or graphic—can have just as great an impact. Oral language—with all the tones and expressions that go with it—engages several senses and both sides of the brain. Written language engages only the eyes and the characters written in linear sequences use mostly the left side of the brain, often shifting the way the brain functions. The result is that as a culture shifts from primarily oral language to written language, the thought patterns of its members shift.

---

[5] It's very similar in meaning to the words *Shalom*, *Sala'am*, and *Shanti-Om*, without the implied action of those words

Tibet Becomes Buddhist

One of humanity's most interesting stories, little known outside the world of lamas and lamaseries, illustrates this process. It's the story of how Tibet came to be Buddhist and what it did next.

It seems that in the century following the blessed prophet Mohammed's revelation of the Q'uran to his people on the Arabian peninsula, there were scholars and mystics in the mountains north of India who realized that Islam was expanding rapidly and would soon be invading the lands they lived in. They talked quietly among themselves of the potential and wondered how best to prepare. They prayed and meditated on the subject, holding the intention for a solution. Some of them began to train disciples from lands to the East in order to maintain their teachings in those places during the difficult centuries ahead.

It happened that the king of Tibet, a practitioner of the ancient *Bon* shamanic tradition, had a dream in which he saw that a wave of bearded men would sweep across India and destroy all signs of Buddhism and much of Hinduism. Though he was not trained in either tradition, he was centered in the ways of balance and harmony on this Earth and he knew, in his heart of hearts, that such destruction must not be allowed to happen.

So he sent messengers into India to find a living Buddha, an awakened one (which is what the term *buddha* means, who would be able to keep the tradition alive. They came back with one name on their lips: Padmasambhava. And so the king of Tibet sent a royal invitation to this man whom he'd never met, who followed a practice that was not his own, to come to Tibet and keep that practice alive.

Well, of course, Padmasambhava was so well centered in wisdom and so far-seeing that he knew the invitation was on its way, and went out to meet the royal party. He told them he would come to Tibet and teach the Buddhist way but they would have to develop a written form of the Tibetan language for him to do so. The king agreed.

And so for the next 25 years, Padmasambhava walked around Tibet, teaching the native people the Noble Truths and the Middle Way that had been taught by Prince Gautama in

Northern India over a 1,500 years before. At the same time, the king and his family developed a written form of the Tibetan language that could make sense of these truths and set them down for all to read for generations to come. In the process, the two together transformed the country, unifying a spiritual practice with a governmental structure through the creation of a written language.

Then they embarked on an even bigger project. Once they had everything in place, they sent messengers into all the countries of Asia and Europe to learn those languages and find healers who really knew how to heal. These healers were then invited into Tibet so they might be interviewed and their healing wisdom could be written down and saved, as well. One or two of those healers chose to stay in Tibet and their descendants have contributed to the lineages of healers and doctors in that country, ever since.

Finally, around 900 c.e., the Moghuls began their long-expected invasion of India, and Tibet closed its borders. No more would people travel freely through their lands. There was too much at stake—the wisdom they had preserved was too precious for thoughtless mobs to steal and burn. They built their lives around maintaining that wisdom.

And so it remained until the 1950s, when China, always a difficult neighbor, overpowered the Tibetans and began the systematic destruction of all that had been preserved for so many years.

Fortunately, a precious few lamas, doctors, and teachers escaped into India and Nepal and moved out into the world. With them came an equally precious few of those written documents, and a remarkable store of other writings locked in their memories, to be written down and shared once again. So, today, in almost every land, the ancient Buddhist practices are being restored—and with them, much of the healing wisdom that Tibetans have learned from those ancient healers, as well.[6]

---

[6] A detailed account may be found in Yeshe Tsogyal's *The Lotus-Born: The Life Story of Padmasambhava.*

Because a king had a dream and, with the help of a very wise man, created a written language, they managed to preserve something he knew was good, and a whole new way of life was born. What had been a shamanic, herd-centered culture became a Buddhist, monastery-centered culture, with shamanic practices buried in the essential Buddhist way of thinking and living. They were no longer the same, but because they changed, the whole world has access to that wisdom, today.

The Language of Sacred Scripture

But this very fact raises an interesting question: if reading a written language shifts us into a different mental framework from that of hearing spoken language, what does that say about the written form of sacred scriptures and the cultures that depend on them?

The Hebrew Bible—*Torah, Psalms, Proverbs,* and the chronicles of judges, prophets, and kings—brought many things into this world. It was the first writing to give us a linear story of a people, placing them on a specific journey with a specific timeline. In so doing, it introduced the idea of progress to humanity. It was also the first to give an explanation for the source of the laws by which the people were governed. In so doing it let us see that laws may be defined—and even changed. Beyond all that, it's the only writing that actually chronicles the process by which joint leadership by men and women in Middle Eastern culture became leadership by men alone (more on that later). But it, too, changed its people, and perhaps not entirely for the better.

There are six major sets of sacred texts in the world, and thousands of oral spiritual traditions. The texts were written in Sanskrit, Persian, Hebrew, Greek, and Arabic (in chronological order)[7] and have been translated into virtually every other human language. All of these written languages appear to have derived from the Aryan culture, with its traditions of conquering indigenous peoples and building empires. They have many terms in

---

[7] The Chinese texts, in the form of the *Tao te Ching* and the works of Kung fu tse (Confucius), are not considered sacred scripture in the same way as the others. They are specifically taught as wise guidelines for living, not as divine revelation.

common and all the texts tend to focus on heroes who accomplish great things by being attentive to their divine guidance.

We can see, though, an interesting shift over time as we study the experiences described in them. In the earliest, Sanskrit and Persian, texts the relationship between divinity and humanity is almost seamless—there's virtually no separation, and conversations are easy and frequent. By contrast, in the Hebrew texts, there's often a barrier between the heroes and their divine Source. And in the Greek Jewish and Christian testaments, there's a vast chasm between the people writing and being written to and the divinity they seek to know. Then, by the time the blessed prophet Mohammed has his revelation in Arabic, the assumption is that only he is capable of receiving input from the divine Source. Finally, when Martin Luther began translating the Christian sacred text into common languages, particularly among English speaking Americans, the Bible itself began to be worshipped as the living Word, the only available source of Truth.

Meanwhile, cultures with oral traditions continue to feel a deep, ongoing communication with the Power and Presence that is the Source of all that is.

The question becomes clear: is it possible that the very act of learning about spirituality through the written word separates us from what we seek? Does the linear stream of letters on a page separate us from the everywhere-present One?

Sanskrit and Hebrew

Prior to the Hebrew *Torah*, there were written descriptions of specific people and their lives, like a Pharaoh in Egypt, or an emperor or hero in Sumeria, or there were timeless stories of discovery and accomplishment, and poems describing the wonders of divinity, like the Vedas in India, but there were no historical progressions of a culture, and certainly no written explanations for how a people came to be who they were and where they were located.

Something changed with *Torah*. It may be the writing itself.

The historical development of Hebrew as a written language, and the relationship between Sanskrit, the language of the invading Aryan/Caucasians which is now the written foundation for the Hindu and Buddhist spiritual traditions, and Hebrew, the language of the invading Semites which is now the written foundation for Judaism, is not at all clear.

One possible indication that Hebrew is related to the Indo-European language is that there are significant similarities between the forms of some of the letters in the two languages. Note, for example the *Mem* in Hebrew and the m in Sanskrit or the Hebrew *Pe* compared to the p in Sanskrit, or the k and the *Koph*—and this is with the joining line across the tops of the letters in the Sanskrit, which is their modern form, after thousands of years of separate development.

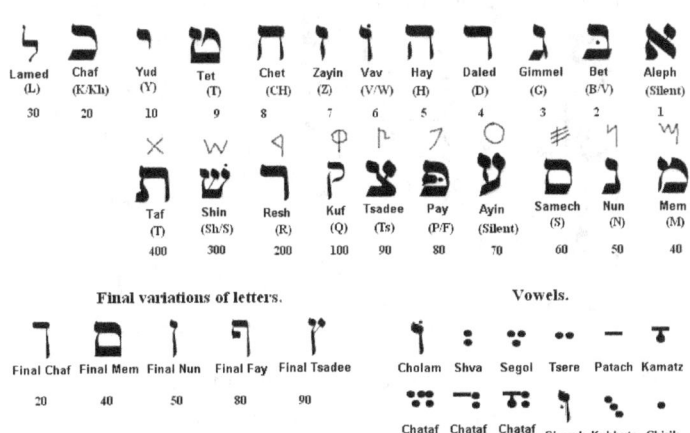

Also, there are parts of India, particularly around Kashmir, where many words could be derived from either language. For example:

HEBREW	KASHMIRI
El Shaddai (The Almighty)	Saday; Sada (Shiva)
Ha-Kadosh (The Holy One)	Hakh-e-Kheda (God's Duty)

And there are many other similar words, mostly related to religion, leading some to suggest that a group of Hebrew-speaking Jews or Christians migrated to Kashmir and interbred with the locals, sharing their spiritual terms.

Nonetheless, scholars hold that the written form of Hebrew is far closer to the symbolic languages of Egypt and the Negev than to the Iranian (Aryan) cuneiform that ultimately became the Greek and Latin alphabets. One comparison is illustrated below:

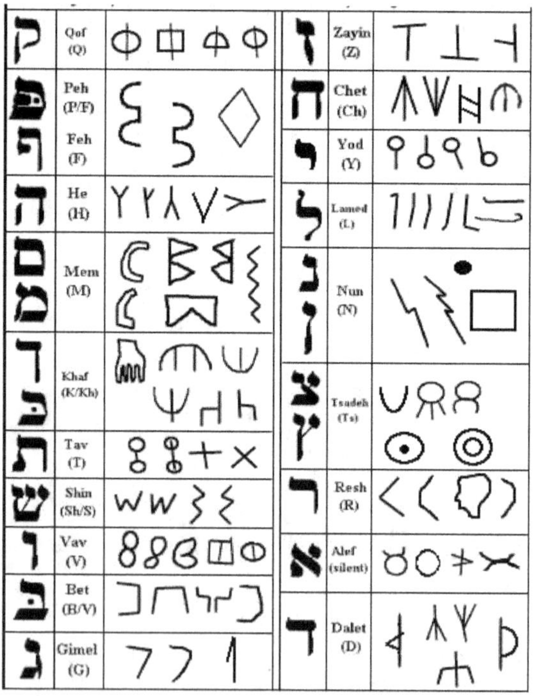

As a result, most linguists place Hebrew within the African language group rather than the Indo-European language group.

This is in spite of the fact that *Torah*, the oldest stories about the Hebrew-speaking people, states clearly that they identify themselves as part of the Indo-European family: Abraham is from Ur in Mesopotamia; his wife was buried in a Hittite (Aryan) tomb; Jacob who becomes Israel returns to the region around Ur to find a wife. In fact, it's not until Israel's son Joseph is sold as a slave and becomes Pharaoh's right-hand man that they move into Egyptian Africa.

This fact raises a significant question, if the written form of Hebrew is more like the African writing than like the Indo-European, is that when the spoken Hebrew of a shamanic tribe became the written Hebrew of an urbanized people? Is it the centuries in Egypt that set the Israelites up to fail to enter the Promised Land? Did they become urbanized, left-brained consumers, unable to maintain the full-brained, holistic connection with the All that was necessary to fully experience what was offered?

Hebrew as a Living Language

"Most of us, even good scholars among us, read Genesis from a tone-deaf perspective, not with the eye and the ear that is attuned to Qabala to the receiving of the incredibly complex cosmic history which is codified within the projective resonance of the Hebrew letters. Read with the musician's or Qabalistic ear, a Biblical account is not only the record of the wanderings of a Semitic tribe and their patriarchs, it is... " a concealed record of the actual events of the projection of the Cosmic Drama into the biosphere"
~ Jean Houston [8]

Milt Markewitz

This chapter isn't steeped in research or any deep understanding of the Hebrew language as spoken in either ancient or modern times. Instead it is my search for something that I found missing from Carlos Suares' *The Cipher of Genesis* which, in my mind, is necessary to further understand the integral connections between language and life—particularly the stories that define our Cosmology.

Suares assumes that ancient Hebrew, like many other languages such as Sanskrit, Chinese, and many indigenous peoples' languages, were initially felt and heard as energies emanating from the Universe by their respective shamanistic leaders.

He also believes that Judaism lost its essence when it created an alphabet and written words. In them the energy of the characters was largely obscured, he suggests, and all the interpretations that have followed must necessarily lack the essence that comes from being energetically connected with all life, the Earth and the Universe.

Let's explore that idea further.

---

[8] quoting Suares' *Cipher of Genesis*, p. 26, on the website:
http://www.psyche.com/psyche/txt/powers_of_genesis.html

If one were to go online or check out a Hebrew dictionary, one would probably find something like this:

Or, if one were interested in the relationship between the Hebrew letters and numbers, one would find something like this:

1	א	10	י	100	ק
2	ב	20	כ,ך	200	ר
3	ג	30	ל	300	ש
4	ד	40	מ,ם	400	ת
5	ה	50	נ,ן		
6	ו	60	ס		
7	ז	70	ע		
8	ח	80	פ,ף		
9	ט	90	צ,ץ		

Suares' model (next page) goes beyond either of these traditional approaches, making it clear that the numerical value points to something far greater than simply a factor of ten. Suares combines the 22 basic Hebrew characters plus the 5 characters that appear differently when they are at the end of a word to form a 27 character letter-number system that he then articulates in a 3x9 matrix. The three rows represent three of the four Worlds of the Qabala—the mystical arm of Judaism—which for me represent three realities. These are: Archetypal (relating to underlying structures of matter and energy emerging as ideal forms), Existential (relating to human experience), and Cosmological (relating to the fundamentals of all being)—each with an apparently different scientific basis. The nine columns appear to be life processes—perhaps all that is necessary and sufficient to support all life processes.

As we were studying Suares' book and the matrix he develops in it, several questions arose. The most fascinating one for me (and the motivation for this book) was:

> Could these 3 of the 4 Worlds so prominent in Qabala be based on realities we now know exist, each with its own established science?

This question emerges out of the following observations:

- Suares' description of the Archetypal World fits descriptions of the implicate order out of which form emerges;
- His Existential World is our well understood observable, tangible experiences; and
- His Cosmological World, the source for all there is, isn't generally thought of as a reality, but what is more real than the emergent, evolutionary process in which living systems adapt, flourish and recompose?
- The 4th World, intrinsic to the study of the Qabala, is called the *Ein Sof* and is beyond comprehension.

Other questions that emerged from our study of Suares' text were:

- Does each of the 9 columns represent a Life Process that when combined with the other 8 Life Processes is all that is necessary and sufficient to create and sustain life?
- If the above question is true, then ancient Hebrew, like many other ancient languages, is a Living Language that reveals deep insights into the blessings bestowed on all life.
- If the last 9 characters are Cosmological, shouldn't they drive the Genesis stories—the first book of the Torah that is Jewish cosmology?
- Are there patterns that relate the 3 levels—specifically does the Cosmological create the Archetypal?
- Is it possible that our current Existential behaviors modify Cosmology, and
- Can we point to a portion in our sacred writings where this happens?
- How does a 'Living Language' contribute to the vitality of the culture that speaks it?
- How is the language itself alive in terms of its own organic qualities?

The answers we arrived at contributed greatly to the creation of this book.

Numbers & Worlds

You may have noticed that each character in the alphabet has a number associated with it:

- the Archetypal are numbered 1 through 9;
- the Existential 10 through 90; and
- the Cosmological 100 through 900.

These numbers are often used in a process called Gematria, a form of numerology, in which the values of each of the characters in a word are totaled, and special meaning is applied to words that have the same total. So the characters not only make up words that have meaning, they make up numbers that have meaning, as well. Using Gematria in English, the letters are lined up in rows of nine (the last row having only 8 letters) and assigned a value between 1 and 9. In Hebrew the letters are already associated with values, far beyond the number 9, and the higher the value, the more exalted the concept being represented.

Emergent Patterns derived from Suares' Work[9]

Through the study group and in conversations with my mentors, I began to integrate my own understandings of Jewish life as a cultural phenomenon, as well as Living Systems theory, through the view of the Hebrew language that Suares offers.

I particularly appreciated the "worlds" that he defined. I find that having worlds that are based on levels of reality, each with their own unique scientific construct, makes much more sense and is more informative than the human attributes—Physical, Mental, Emotional, and Spiritual—that are usually assigned to each of the 4 worlds.

---

[9] What follows is the teaching that Ken Roffmann and I used in the workshop the last time we were together.

My opinion is that for the most part the Jewish people have lost touch with our Cosmology, and live primarily out of our Exodus story rather than our own story of our beginnings. As such we have lost some of our appreciation and love of life, and dwell in grief for what we have lost. I view grief and love as being opposite sides of the same coin, but not as a duality. Every state blended with love is always the prevailing or grounding paradigm.

So, from the perspective of Suares' model, I took another look at two powerful Hebrew texts. First, I looked in the Creation Story for the patterns of Cosmological characters for revelation regarding the evolution of life. Second, I let the Cosmological characters that preceded and were imbedded in "The Binding of Isaac" inform my understanding of what I believe now is a fundamentally misunderstood story. My learning from the Creation patterns follows, and 'The Binding of Isaac' is in a later chapter.

The Genesis Patterns

Working with Suares' idea that certain Hebrew characters are associated with the Cosmological aspect of reality while others evoke the Archetypes (life processes) and the experiential aspects, then the macro-pattern throughout Genesis is that characters associated with the Cosmological World combine to form Archetypal (life) processes that then become the 'soil' from which the experiences in our Existential World emerge as outcomes.

To help quicken the recognition of characters for those not familiar with the Hebrew, I will use the following code:

> Cosmological characters are in a **large, bold** font;

> Archetypal processes are in a medium-size font;

> Existential outcomes are in a smaller, underlined gray font.

I began with the major terms in the Book of Genesis: *Baruch, Shalom,* and *Eretz,* as follows.

Baruch

Baruch is the Hebrew word for blessing. My reading of Suares' chart says that the Cosmic Universal Life, seen in the final *Kaf*, and Cosmic Order, seen in *Raysh*, create an ultimate blessing, Archetypal perfect order, *Bayt*.

Final Kaf 500   Raysh 200   Bayt 2

My interpretation is that we are blessed with absolute perfect order that either exists when everything is biodegradable or when we assume that even our plastics and other materials are biodegradable over a very long period of time.

Shalom

Shalom, usually translated as "Peace be with you," is the word that helped me understand Mahatma Gandhi's definition of peace as presented to his grandson Arun, as described earlier in this book. This is how it looks in this framework:

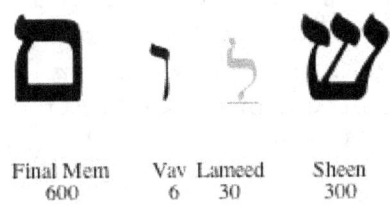

Final Mem 600   Vav Lameed 6 30   Sheen 300

The Cosmological *Sheen* and *final Mem* create the Archetypal capacity for fertilization, *Vav*, from which Existential organic life, *Lammed*, emerges.

Eretz

Eretz, meaning Earth, our planetary home, follows the same pattern of combining the two Cosmological characters *final Tsadde*, sensuality and beauty, with *Raysh*, Order and Structure, to create *Aleph*, the Archetypal Life-Death-Life continuum.

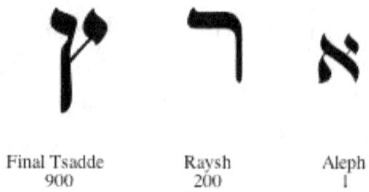

Final Tsadde 900   Raysh 200   Aleph 1

Other Terms

There are several other patterns worth noting. For example, there appear to be patterns of specific characters being repeated over and over again such as in the Beatitudes where almost every word ends in a *final Noun*. Does this mean that each one of the Beatitudes is based upon a Cosmological Possibility?

Or, in the *Kadish*, the Jewish prayer for the deceased, 7 words in one passage begin with *Vav*, the symbol of Archetypal fertilization. Is this whole passage, then, about new life emerging from death?

Torah

Torah is not a word used in Genesis, but is a foundational term for all Jewish people. It has a little different pattern in that there are two Cosmological and two Archetypal characters. While studying the books of *Torah* with Rabbi Aryeh, I asked him if he could articulate the meaning of the word *Torah*. His response was that it means 'The Essence', and I found this to be a very satisfying answer that seems to be confirmed by the following pattern.

Hay 5   Raysh 200   Vav 6   Tav 400

Here the Archetypal *Vav*, Impregnation and Fertilization, and *Hay*, Universal Life, emerge from the Cosmological *Tav*, Birthing, and *Raysh*, Order and Structure.

There also appear to be passages with patterns that relate the three levels—specifically the Cosmological creating the Archetypal, and the Existential influencing the Cosmological in an organic, evolutionary process.

More Patterns

One link between the Existential and the Cosmological is the 5 letter-numbers that transform into Final letters. When Suares describes the transformations of *Kaf* (20), *Mem* (40) and *Noun* (50) into their *final Kaf* (500), *Mem* (600) and *Noun* (700) he writes, "those (letter-) numbers acquire such cosmic values when they unfold in human beings."[10] Clearly he supports my idea of the Existential elevating to the Cosmological.

Also, it should be recognized that each letter-number is made up of other letter-numbers and they thus carry those energies as part of their own. For example, the word for the symbol *Aleph* is spelled *Aleph-Lammed-final Phay*, and so carries its own energy as a symbol, plus that of *final Phay*, Cosmological Energy, and *Lammed*, Existential Organic Life. And, of course, each of the 'secondary' letter-numbers is composed of 'tertiary' letter-numbers, e.g. *Lammed* is composed of *Lammed-Mem-Dalet*. The progression, and thus the infusion of energy, is never-ending.[11]

Because language shapes the stories that formulate some of our deepest beliefs, and the stories being lived today by the most influential individuals, corporations, and nations aren't sustainable; we must do whatever we can to recreate our stories. In the words of the Ecuadorian, Achuar People when asked by the North American founders of the Pachamama movement what is will take for the planet to become sustainable, "We must change the dream of the North."[12] Inherent in such a statement is an understanding of both the dream that we are living and the dream to which we must transform.

---

[10] Suares, Carlos, *The Cipher of Genesis: The Original Code of the Qabala*, p. 63

[11] A description, hypertext, of each of the letter-numbers can be found at http://www.psyche.com/psyche/autiot/hyper_autiot.html

[12] http://www.pachamama.org/about/origin-story

These transformations are the 'Paradigm Shifts' referred to in the Joanna Macy chart presented in the Introduction to this book, and the 'Systemic Understanding' necessary to make these shifts. beginning to emerge in Western science, is embedded in the wisdom of the ancient languages.

Three Worlds

Ruth L. Miller

Prologue

One of the wonderful unfoldings in my life has been the many opportunities I get to integrate scientific and spiritual understandings in books and lectures. Most times I get to do this within the Western, Judeo-Christian norm of U.S. culture, but one day in 2005 I was asked to stretch a bit and expand my understanding of meditation methods to include Tibetan traditional healing methods. Robert Bruce Newman was a long-time student of both Chogyam Trungpa Rinpoche, the ardent young teacher who woke Americans up to the existence of Tibetan meditation, and Didjum Rinpoche, the head of the Nyingma lineage of Tibet and hence meditation instructor to the Dalai Lama. Robert had founded an organization called Medigrace and was teaching these methods as a way to transform childbirth. He had recently published a book on his Calm Birth method and was being asked by his publisher to do a new book that would expand the methods beyond childbirth.

Robert heard me do a talk in which I was able to explain how it is that the mental healing methods employed by practitioners of Science of Mind can work, and he believed I could explain why and how his Tibetan methods work, as well.

Together, we created *Calm Healing,* a book that the publisher called "a virtual bible of mind-based healing methods."[13] It included a compilation of the research showing the physiological and psychological benefits of meditation as well as a model of the body that explains how and why shifting our mental activity must change the structure and function of the material body.

---

[13] Grossinger, Richard, from the Foreword to *Calm Healing: Methods for Era III Medicine,* North Atlantic Press, 2006.

We developed that model by integrating the traditional Western models with the traditional Tibetan model, which, thankfully, is one of the teachings that survived the Tibetan exile. Their model of reality is embedded in the ancient Sanskrit *Vedas* and the commentaries on them, called the *Upanishads,* texts that are also sacred foundations of Hinduism, but it's developed most fully in the Tibetan school of Vajrayana Buddhism.

The Trikaya

The teaching is that there are 3 kinds of *kaya,* or realms of existence, that may be found within each person as well as throughout the cosmos. They are both abstract ideas and experiences; both intellectual and physico-emotional, and all that is may be understood in terms of them.

The foundation of the 3 kinds, *Dharmakaya,* means "truth body" or "body of absolute nature." This is the empty or open nature of being inseparable from pure awareness. In terms of Western physics it can be defined as the quantum field within the atomic nature of the corporal form, the subatomic void of pure potential, from which the universe and its infinite forms emerge. The Dharmakaya is the nonlocal, universal field, the basis of the human being's unlimited nature—timeless, deathless, unchanging. It may correspond to what Georges Gurdjieff called essence, the fundamental nature of being, and modern Buddhists call "the ground of being." It's what physicist Amit Goswami calls the consciousness that pervades and creates the material universe.

Spontaneously arising from the Dharmakaya is the *Sambhogakaya*, which is the body of communication, the connecting form, the realm of David Bohm's implicate order and Carl Jung's archetypes. Francesca Fremantle, in her book *Luminous Emptiness*, describes it in terms of light:

> Light radiates from the emptiness of dharmakaya as the five colors of the five kinds of knowledge. It appears in shining rainbow clouds, in glowing circles, in scintillating pinpoints, and dazzling rays of light. Then the five colors crystallize into... divine forms... made entirely of light; they arise out of light and dissolve back into light. This is the realm of sacred vision... the bridge between emptiness and form: emptiness

displaying itself as form; form revealing itself to be emptiness.[14]

The *Nirmanakaya*, or manifest nature, is the actual physical body energy appearing as matter, to act in the realm of matter. The term literally means "body of emanation" because it emanates from the Sambhogakaya. Fremantle says:

> The experience of the *trikaya* can be found everywhere; it is a continual presence in our lives. The *dharmakaya* is present in the sense of openness, the source and background of all phenomena. The *sambhogakaya* is present in the sense of energy bursting forth, the sacred, magical quality of life. And the *nirmanakaya* is present in the sense of phenomena continually arising, imper-manent yet vividly apparent.[15]

Within this threefold structure, Buddhist research says that each sentient being has 3 "doors"—body, speech, and mind—through which our deeds, thoughts, and words work in the world. Body refers to the manifest, material form and corresponds to the Nirmanakaya. "It is the outward expression in material form of our mind and energy."[16] Speech corresponds to Sambhogakaya: energy, emotion, and communication. It refers to both the outward sounds and the inner emotions from which they emanate. It is the essential processes by which life occurs. The invisible, formless mind corresponds to the Dharmakaya, including all our thoughts, perceptions, feelings, and reactions, and encompassing the Western ideas of heart and mind, together.[17]

The Western equivalent to *trikaya* would be "spirit, mind, body" or, in the occult teachings, the "etheric," "subtle," and "material" worlds and bodies.

Clearly, this structure parallels the matrix that Suares offers and Milt is exploring here. Three aspects of being; 3 levels of un-

---

[14] Francesca Fremantle, *Luminous Emptiness*, 2001, p, 178
[15] ibid., 75
[16] ibid., 180
[17] This material is drawn from the new edition of our book called *Empowered Care, Mind-Body Medicine Methods*, published as a Medigrace Book by Portal Center Press in 2012.

folding: cosmological, archetypal, existential, each with its own science. If we were open to the experience, what might we be?

Accessing the Cosmological

The Buddhist tradition emerged out of the Hindu tradition, so there are significant overlaps in terminology and practice. Gautama was, after all, a Hindu prince who found a way to use Hindu practices to transcend the limitations of Hinduism.

One of those practices is meditation. One variation on the practice of meditation is chanting.

In chanted meditation, the practitioner repeats a sound over and over until the sound and the repetition fade away and the only thing that's left is Pure Awareness. In Tibetan this state is called *rigpa*, and it is the direct experience of the Dharmakaya. The particular sound that is used most often is the sound that Krishna tells Prince Arjuna to focus on in the Vedic text, *Bhagavad Gita*. That sound is *Om*.

In the ' (the Hindu equivalent of the Christian New Testament or Muslim *Q'uran*, usually translated as "Song of God") Krishna says that he is *Om*, the source of all and the all, the essence and the existence, that which is, was, and ever shall be—and many other such descriptors. In short, it becomes clear that Krishna is the embodiment of the Dharmakaya and that to be free of the limitations of body, social role, and craving, one must focus on that aspect of being until it's the only experience.

This is the practice that so many images and recordings of Tibetan monks illustrate. And this is the primary link between Tibet and India, today.

The practice is purely experiential—no intellect involved—and may be the link between all spiritual traditions. It may be the oldest of spiritual traditions. No matter if we're Hindu, Christian, Muslim, Jew, Taoist, or mystic-of-the-forest-or-desert: we speak the name that we understand as power-presence-wisdom-essence until that is all we are experiencing. The word takes form and the form is the word and all are held in the unnamable One.

PART 2

STORIES

"How did the creek get the song? asked the man. I don't know, answered the elder, but sometimes songs are like that. If they don't have anyone to sing them, they'll give themselves over to a creek for safekeeping. ... Many things such as songs, dances, stories, and prayers, that our culture sees as strictly human fabrication, seem to be viewed by some traditional cultures as entities that exist on their own….. much of what people need to know is seen as residing in the world around them, with a mind and spirit of its own; in certain situations such knowledge gives itself over to people." ~ *Malcolm Margolin*[18]

---

[18] Malcom Margolin, 'Indian Pedagogy', *Sacred Fire Magazine*, Issue Six, p.18

The Binding of Isaac

Milt Markewitz

Avraham's Revelation

I first noticed the pattern of two Cosmological characters combining into what I believed was creating an Archetypal process when I was creating a *Midrash* (which means "an interpretation") of the Genesis story, "The Binding of Isaac." In the story there's a line that's generally translated as "Avraham journeyed from Kadish to Shir." I'd heard it interpreted as either he literally traveled, or that it was a time of introspection.

Reading the story from the perspective of the Hebrew letters being used, I felt it was much more the latter. It seemed to be describing Avraham's profound revelation of the Cosmic forces that created the capacity for birth, as shown by the *Dallet* in the word *Kadish*, and the Cosmic forces that created the capacity for fertilization, the *Vav* in the word *Shir*.[19]

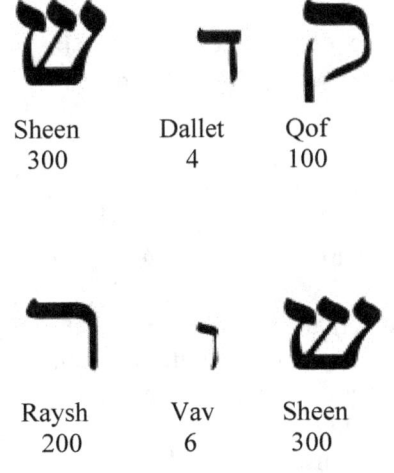

| Sheen | Dallet | Qof |
| 300 | 4 | 100 |

| Raysh | Vav | Sheen |
| 200 | 6 | 300 |

---

[19] Hebrew words are read from right to left, unlike the English left to right.

It seemed to me that the story is telling us that when these two capacities were combined, Avraham could understand the Archetypal Life-Death-Life continuum, *Aleph*, and the Archetypal Universal Life, *Hay*, from the combination of which emerges all manifest experience, all that is Existential.

This famous Biblical story is generally understood to be about G*d asking Abraham, Isaac's father, to sacrifice Isaac. The name of this Torah portion is *Aiqida* and when we look at the Hebrew spelling, there is both the recurring pattern and insight into the essence of the story.

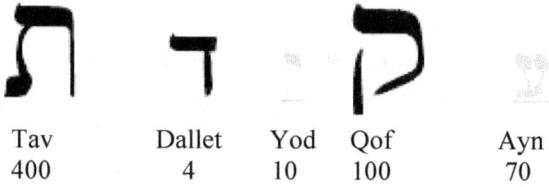

Tav	Dallet	Yod	Qof	Ayn
400	4	10	100	70

The 2 Cosmological forces *Tav*—birth, and *Qof*--the life-death-life cycle, combine to create Archetypal birth--*Dallet*, from which Existential possibility--*Ayn*, and life-death-life—*Yod*, emerge. Clearly we have a story about birth, driven by cosmological forces, and full of life and possibilities.

The Story

In this narrative I'll be speaking as Abraham and using the Hebrew names; Isaac is *Yitzhhaq*, and mine is *Avraham*.

Prologue

As you probably know I'm known as the 'father' of the Abrahamic Traditions, and it is recognized by all that I had a very close relationship with G*d. All this is true, but perhaps not as you may think. G*d didn't speak to me in the commonly understood way that two people communicate, but instead I was in constant communion with G*d through Nature and through an energetic language that emanated from the universe and resonated with all there is. For me this is communion—relationship with all there is through mind, body and spirit. And I was not alone in that. The community from which I came also spoke this language—we were what you call mystics, and revelation abounded among us. Prior to my journey with Yitzhhaq, I had experienced the profound revelation mentioned above, as well as the responsibility to embed this revelation into the genetic makeup of the generations of peoples to follow.

In brief, the revelation was an understanding that G*d's Cosmological powers create the Archetypal capacities for fertilization and birth in such a way that life could perpetuate itself in a perfectly ordered, sensually beautiful, evolutionary emergent way.

Revelation was facilitated by our Hebrew language, in which each character is a sacred geometry of sound and shape—a symbiotic energy with every other character. The language kept us deeply connected to place both locally and globally, as well as to time—past, present and future—from which emerged the ethics of how we must live each day. It was this language that informed us of our cosmology, and our responsibility to maintain the balance and harmony with which we are blessed.

It became clear to me that there are several Archetypal processes created by Cosmological powers, and it is these processes that are necessary and sufficient for the perpetuation of life. All life has been blessed with these extraordinary processes.

How was all this wisdom to be captured and passed on? I quickly realized that I must take a son to the sacred mount, *Adonoi Jireh*. Yitzhhaq–open, sensible, balanced–was my choice.

We spoke of the journey, the impending challenges, and the responsibilities. Our 4-day, 3-night journey to *Adonoi Jireh* would be physically difficult, yet our preparation was almost entirely spiritual. We initially traveled with two other men who carried some supplies, but our plan was to travel the last two days alone, during which time we would live off the blessings of this arid land.

Yitzhhaq the Potential DNA of an Enlightened People

Initially as we walked, I shared what had been revealed to me. All the while Yitzhhaq saw, heard, smelled, absorbed, and connected with everything. Then at night, with a sky filled with astrological wonder, he journeyed into the Cosmos and felt its welcome attraction.

The first night, Yitshhaq was quiet. He would ask a question from time to time, and I could feel in the silence that he was reflecting and synthesizing all that he was learning.

In the middle of the second day, we left our fellow travelers so that we could travel on alone and experience the subtle blessings that emerge from a land that otherwise looks as if it has little to offer.

That evening Yitzhhaq shared with me his understanding of the paradox of our planet, so powerful and balanced, yet so fragile. He spoke of a narrow bandwidth in which species including ourselves can live, and how we rely on *Eretz*, our Earth, to cleanse and heal. He discerned the finiteness of the planet, the possibilities of a future in which we might lose touch with the essence of life; that we might not understand that if *Eretz*, the Earth, was to take care of us then we must take care of her. He also shared that there is a spark of divinity in all of life that must be fully appreciated or we will do great harm to our environment and subsequently our social order.

We walked all day together delighted with the discoveries we were making. It seemed as if we were drawn to everything we needed. Yitzhhaq was particularly good at relying on his sensual connections to the land to intuit how to find food and water.

That night he shared with me his connection with all life, that we have all been blessed with the same basic life processes, and that we feed each other as we recompose in a life-death-life continuum. Yitzhhaq finished with the following statement,

The very essence of life has been revealed to me along with the understanding that life is not deterministic. We have choice, and with choice we have responsibilities. It is through the understanding of life that a clear ethic emerges and becomes integral to every seed. We must not lose touch with the understanding of sufficiency, and sharing that which is scarce. This knowing and way of being can only be present when we discern *Adonoi*, G*d, as the essence that resides in all life.

It occurred to me as Yitzhhaq spoke that we must never lose our symbolic language of life, or our oral tradition, because it is through the language that we are able to deeply understand the revelation.

Before we slept that night, Yitzhhaq spoke these most incredible thoughts, "I believe that I fully understand who each of us is and our relationship to the birth of a new peoples. You, 'Avraham'

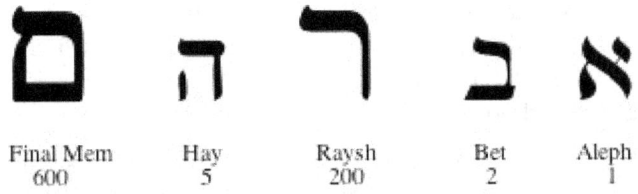

Final Mem	Hay	Raysh	Bet	Aleph
600	5	200	2	1

come from the Cosmic Order *(Raysh)* of life and have become the Cosmic Enlightened Human (final *Mem)*, the archetype of Universal Life *(Hay)*, and living life with a complete acceptance of death *(Aleph)*. And I, Yitzhhaq,

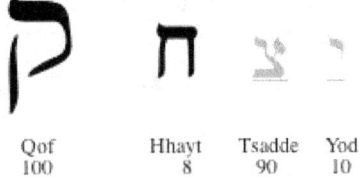

Qof	Hhayt	Tsadde	Yod
100	8	90	10

understand my own mission to be the seed for the generations of fully living people, *Yod*, that manifest their connection to mystery and sensual beauty, *Tsadde*, where all decisions are ethically grounded, *Hhayt*, all emanating from the Cosmic Life-Death-Life force, *Qof*. The *Yod* in my name and being flows from your *Aleph*, and the seed that I produce must not be a *Yod* that just exists, but one that lives life to the fullest by embracing and being in concert with all the blessings that are life."

I slept a wonderful sleep that night having had one of those moments of deep appreciation for my son who had transformed from being a young adult to being a peer in terms of wisdom, compassion, and leadership. Yitzhhaq had become an enlightened *Yod*, whose seed was capable of passing that appreciation of life to all the generations.

We rose early the next morning to complete our journey. We were unclear if there was to be more revelation, or how we might know if we had passed, or not passed, these most arduous and crucial tests. If we had not passed, then there could be no new people. The seed would be terminated, essentially aborted as it is in Nature if a fetus isn't prepared for birth. We were prepared for that judgment.

The cosmic forces got stronger and stronger as we approached the summit. I felt an energy the likes of which I'd never felt. I could hardly breathe, and I felt as if I was detached from my body.

I became aware of two new, very powerful, resonating forces. They were both the cosmological forces of *Qof, Raysh*.

The first, *Bikarna*, regrettably translated as 'horns', emanated from *Eretz*, the Earth. *Bikarna* is a most powerful word not only because of the Cosmological characters, but because from its two Archetypal processes Order and Impregnation emerges Existential Universal Life all part of the Life-Death-Life recomposing process.

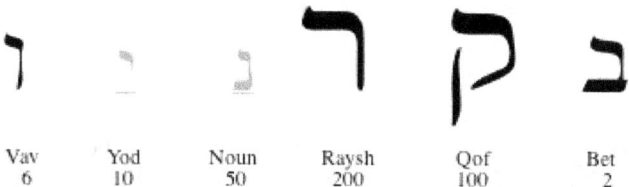

Vav	Yod	Noun	Raysh	Qof	Bet
6	10	50	200	100	2

The second, *Vyekra*, seemed to be coming from the heavens and is translated as a 'calling' of the angels. These two words are almost mirror images. *Vyekra* has at its Archetypal processes Fertilization and the Life-Death-Life Continuum from which emerges Existential Life-Death-Life Continuum.

Aleph	Raysh	Qof	Yod	Vav
1	200	100	10	6

Both of us recognized these two forces, and as we became comfortable with them, they seemed to soften. Harmony replaced what we'd first perceived as dissonance. This final revelation was God's acceptance of Yitzhhaq as the seed for perpetuating the belief system that has become Judaism.

Yitzhhaq and I shared a simple prayer before we departed *Adonoi Jireh*. It is a prayer of thankfulness that each of us appreciated more fully then ever before. It is a prayer each of you has often said, perhaps without meaning before, but hopefully with great meaning now. We said 'Amen', a vibrant set of shamanic characters:

Final Noun   Mem   Aleph
700   40   1

Of all the infinite possibilities and combinations of what might be, the final *Noun* creates this beautiful Life-Death-Life Continuum... *Aleph*, we give thanks for this moment and what has been birthed... *Mem*.

Epilogue

Hebrew is no longer a shamanic language—the characters exist as letters but their energy and meaning has been lost. Also, our oral tradition has been largely replaced with the written word. Without the language and the conversations, we've lost the capacity for deep understanding. We read the Torah as if you know it is Truth, but the Truth has been obscured by written words that lack energy, and, paradoxically, an ambiguity that is necessary if our stories are to retain their essence.

"The Binding of Yitzhhaq" is one very small example of what we've lost. Virtually every scripture has lost its original meaning, and the problem perpetuated when our interpretations are developed without the wisdom imbedded in the ancient Hebrew.

Please recognize that there are other cultures that have retained their shamanic language, and emanating from their language is a deeply held sense of life being in harmony and balance as well as an appreciation for all life yielding a profound happiness.

I hope you understand that what you may have previously understood as a story about a father being commanded to kill his son is more a story about revelation, and the test of adversity to assure a successful birth and perpetuation. Today some of the essence of the understandings Yitzhhaq/Isaac gained have been retained, and some are lost. What has been retained manifests in your ethical behavior, and your beautiful connections with life that give the sacred places in your life the feeling of deep love and caring.

But there are strong cultural forces that impel us into acting in ways that will deeply harm, perhaps even kill, future generations: our children. From this perspective, the "Binding of Isaac" is a very relevant story for our times. I believe that each of us must find our way to revelation, and to be tested so that we develop our tensile strength and sense of courage.

My suggested starting point is the resurrection of our 'language of life'--Hebrew characters full of the power and energy to create and sustain life. And that we teach it to people of all ages in order to provide the deep understanding that defines the path to revelation, and the emanation of the ethic that guides us. From this understanding will come a different, very enlightened understanding of the Torah.

I thank you for letting me share this with you and let us say *Amen*.

Creation

"In the beginning God created the heavens and the earth. Now the earth was formless and empty, darkness was over the surface of the deep, and the Spirit of God was hovering over the waters. And God said, "Let there be light," and there was light. God saw that the light was good..."
~ Genesis 1:1-4

Milt Markewitz & Batya Podos

While my primary lens for processing Suares' work is discerning Hebrew as a living language by which human experience comes into form, I'm also focused on patterns of the language that might inform our understanding of life. What follows is the first line of Genesis—the first line of the first day of Creation.

As you can see, what was written is a string of characters with no punctuation. Using my code for Suares' matrix of meanings, you can also see that every word in the string has at least one Cosmological letter-number (the larger letters).

Four words in that string are fundamental to the reading: *B'reishit*, *Et*, *Eretz*, and *Hashamaim*.

1) B'reishit,

Tav	Yod	Sheen	Aleph	Raysh	Bayt
400	10	300	1	200	2

This first word of the Old Testament, the Torah, is often translated as "In the Beginning"; sometimes as "In a Beginning"; and to my way of thinking, "In our Beginning". It has three Cosmological characters: *Raysh*, meaning Cosmological Order and Structure; *Sheen*, Cosmological Life (the breath of G*d); and *Tav*, Cosmological Birth. Together they create the Archetypal processes—*Bayt*, which is Order and Structure; and *Aleph*, the Life-Death-Life Continuum—that are necessary to support *Yod* the Existential Life-Death-Life Continuum.

This pattern of Cosmological characters combining to form an Archetypal process occurs over and over again throughout the Genesis story, sometimes with an Existential outcome, but often not.

My tendency is to get the feel for the power of a word by multiplying the numerical values of the Cosmological characters, and I know of no other word as powerful as *B'reishit* with its three Cosmological characters (400x300x200=24,000,000).

2) Et

Tav   Aleph
400   1

Et is found over and over in the Torah, and is usually passed over without thinking or commentary. It's the sign that something or someone is the object of an action. But I believe it is very powerful, because *Aleph* is the 1st letter-number and *Tav* the last letter-number in the basic twenty-two (22) letter-number alphabet.

This combination essentially integrates all the energy of the letter-numbers and bestows it on what comes before and after—it's a form of the "*Alpha* and *Omega*" (First and Last) of the Greek New Testament.

3) Hashamaim

Final Mem	Yod	Mem	Sheen	Hay
600	10	40	300	5

Hashamaim is generally translated as 'The Heaven', but I believe means significantly more. With two Cosmological letter-numbers, *Sheen*, the Breath of G*d, and *final Mem*, the Perfect Seed, combined with Archetypal Universal Life, *Hay*, supporting Existential birth, *Mem*, and the life-death-life cycle, *Yod*. It should also be noted that the *Mem* and *final Mem* exist in the same word, and with it the transformative energy between Existential birth to Cosmic Fertilization. Here's what Suares has to say when he looks at *Shamaim* (without the Ha that he considers a separate word):

> *Shamaim* contains a *Yod* between two *Mem*. This sequence indicates the cosmic movement of *Sheen* acting against *Mayim*, the so called waters: the two *Mem* between which *Yod* is playing against its partner Aleph in the game of existence versus life. *Yod* is all we know and all that exists. And it plays against its very destruction.[20]

4) Eretz

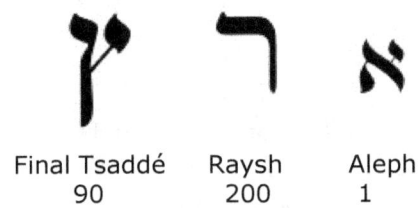

Final Tsaddé	Raysh	Aleph
90	200	1

Eretz was mentioned earlier when I proposed the pattern of two Cosmological forces, *Raysh* and final *Tsadde*, creating the Archetypal process, *Aleph*. What struck me in this last word of the

---

[20] Suares, , ibid, p. 81

first line of the description of Creation is that this is the first final, also called a *sofit* in *Torah*, introducing Cosmological Attraction.

5) Tov

I have also been fascinated by the words, "And it was good" spoken when G*d surveys his work for the day.

Vayt   Vav   Tayt
2   6   9

When reflecting on the product of primarily Cosmological forces that created the subject day, it seems that there must be an architecture in place to support not only what is but what will follow in the Creation Days to follow. Therefore, I opine that, "And it was good", infers that that architecture is in place. As is quoted on the psyche.com website exploring these ideas,

> Tov, *Tayt-Waw-Vayt*, or 9.6.2, or cell-fertilize-container, is eloquent in its description of the repetition of the same container, each seed following its own kind.[21]

From this quote, I think it can be inferred that *tov*, goodness, is a most fundamental building block for all life.

A Creation Story

Batya's Introduction

When I was approached to write for this book, my first response was that I might not be the right person for the job, because I still struggle with Hebrew and I'm not a biblical scholar. I am, however, a lay leader in my synagogue, P'nai Or of Portland, and an ordained *maggid*—a storyteller and teacher in the Jewish tradition. So even though I'm not a scholar, I do know story. I know that the stories we tell to ourselves, to our intimates, and in our communities stitch the narratives of our

---

[21] http://www.psyche.com/psyche/lex//tov-raa.html

individual and communal lives together. It does make a difference which stories we choose and how we choose to tell them.

Most of us in the West, raised within the Abrahamic traditions, know the story of creation as it's written in the sacred texts of Judaism, Christianity and Islam. Most of us, whether we believe it to be true or not, can quote the beginning of the book of Genesis. It's in the common culture.

What is not in the common culture is the understanding that the Hebrew letters are themselves more than just sounds and signs. They are, as Rabbi Lawrence Kushner writes so eloquently, "at the center of a unique spiritual constellation." Each letter has within it the power of creation and is a conduit between humanity and the Divine. When we begin to unpack the original and essential meanings of the Hebrew letters, we get a glimpse into a world that is deeper and more compelling than a simple, literal translation can ever provide.

B'reishit: In a Beginning

In the beforetime there was no breath, no dreaming, only the great emptiness. There was no word, no language even to describe this, no thought even to imagine it. It went on for a long time although there was no time to measure it.

And then something happened. Out of the beforetime there came an inhale. An exhale. A contraction. An explosive expansion. A tearing apart of whatwillbe from whatwasnot.

And that which was the Singularity divided itself into parts: darkness from light, earth from sky, water from land, each broken off from the whole but a part of the whole. And a vessel was made to contain the presence of whatwillbe, to give it shape and to nurture it.

And the whatwillbe became the moon, the stars and the sun. It became plants, trees, moss and lichen. The whatwillbe became the sea and all the creatures that swam, the sky and all the creatures that flew, the landmasses and all the creatures that crawled, walked and ran. And there was a harmony, a balance, a blending of the many parts—each separate but connected, all from the same Source. And the vessel filled with the intensity of so much beingness that it burst into fragments, spilling the light of whatwillbe.

And after a while creatures were created who could recognize the shards of light and collect them, creatures who could repair the vessel. The light of whatwillbe could be gathered and the vessel repaired by the way these creatures chose to live their lives. Everything they need to do this task was provided for them. They only had to recognize it.

There is no word for the time it will take to accomplish this task.

I wrote this creation myth, combining the story from Genesis with a Chassidic creation tale, to see if I could put all the essentials of creation into a few energetic, juicy paragraphs that would reflect my own sense of meaning. As a storyteller, I am aware that the stories I chose to tell, and the words I choose to use when I tell them are as important as any skill or technique I have in the telling.

Choosing Our Story

Batya tells another story by way of explanation of the importance of what we choose to tell:

> When Reb Zuysa's disciple asked him what was the proper way to pray, the Rebbe sent his disciple to visit Chaim the shepherd. "But Rebbe," the disciple complained, "He is a shepherd—what can he know about the Holy Torah and prayer?"
>
> Reb Zuysa replied that Chaim the shepherd was the holiest man he knew, that his prayers reached directly into the ears of Heaven. So the disciple went to find Chaim the shepherd. By the time he reached the fields where Chaim pastured his sheep, it was late and nearly time for evening prayers.
>
> "I have come so you can teach me the proper way to pray," the disciple said. The shepherd stared at him in disbelief. "I am a simple man," he said, "and you are a scholar. There is nothing I can teach you."
>
> "But Reb Zuysa said that your prayers reach the ear of Heaven. There must be something special you do."

But Chaim the shepherd shook his head. "I never went to school. I don't really know any Hebrew, so I pray with what I know. You are welcome to pray with me, but I cannot believe I can teach you anything." With that, Chaim closed his eyes and began to pray, "aleph, beit, gimmel, dalet…"

When he returned home to Reb Zuysa, the disciple related his experience. "I don't understand. The shepherd knew no prayers at all, just the aleph-bet. And yet you say his prayers reach the ear of Heaven. Rebbe, how can this be?"

"It is not the prayer," Reb Zuysa replied. "It is the intention. Within the aleph-bet is the whole world of creation, of every prayer that has ever been or has yet to be. When Chaim the shepherd prays, he sees every letter as a tikkun, a way to repair the world. And that is why his prayers reach the ear of Heaven."

Batya's Commentary

Hebrew is a language of layers. Within each word are worlds of meaning, and theories abound as to which is the correct path to take as we unpack the letters, for we dilute the meanings even as we write them down. If the Hebrew letters represent the profound forces of the universe, we can only scratch the surface through scholarship. What is needed is to experience them, and this is for the realm of the mystics and shamans. I remind myself every time I pick up the text that it is always possible to go deeper, that whatever I discover will be inherently flawed unless I can live within the energetic source of the letters. And still, I begin by working in the way I know and understand, by looking at the meaning of a Hebrew word by looking at its *shoresh*, or root.

The root of *b'reishit* contains the three letters *Raysh, Aleph* and *Sheen* and each has its own mystical meaning. *Raysh* is the cosmic container which is the totality of the universe, *Aleph* is pulsating unbridled force and *Sheen* is cosmic nourishment, the gathering together of all the broken parts.

So the very first word tells the whole story—it's the Big Bang of the Bible. This is when I did my happy dance celebrating the union of Science and Faith. Imagine that within the first few letters of the creation story, we find reference to an immeasurable explosive force, the formation of matter to contain that force, and, within the letter *Aleph*, the expanding and contracting universe! For me, a person who believes that science is proof of G*d, not the antithesis, my unpacking of those first few letters was revelation. The Singularity is split apart, containing and nourishing the universe or creating the container for the universe or both creating and containing simultaneously.

It's like the Chassidic story I referenced in my own retelling of Creation. That story teaches that when G*d created the universe, there was too much light to contain in the vessels created for that purpose, so they split apart, scattering shards of light everywhere. It goes on to remind us that it us our obligation to find those shards of light and return them to the Source, and that we should seek out the light even in the darkest places.

The last letter of *B'reishit* is *Tav*, the last letter of the Hebrew alphabet, and it means "true law." It completes the story we read in Torah, from creation to the building of human systems that order society and create civilizations. True law implies ethical conduct, set out for us within the energy of that first big bang, before human beings were even created; it is the way we are to walk before we are even called into being. It presupposes a tendency to be in harmony with each other and with the environment, that we will deal justly and honestly, that we will rush to do good. The stories of our flawed and difficult ancestors in the remaining chapters of Genesis remind us not of how far we have strayed from our original design, but to what we should strive to return.

In the Wilderness

Milt Markewitz & Batya Podos

Milt's Prologue

Over 10 years ago, I was in a Torah class at P'nai Or, our Jewish Renewal Center in Portland, conducted by Rabbi Aryeh Hirschfield and it happened to be the Torah portion that told of Moses asking his father-in-law, *Yitro* (Jethro), for advice. The passage seemed vague to me and I asked Aryeh if we knew precisely the advice that Yitro gave to Moses. He told me what he knew regarding Yitro's advice regarding organization and delegation, and asked me why I found it so interesting. I told him that I was particularly impressed that Moses sought counsel from a non-Jewish source, that there was likely some wisdom regarding how to survive in the desert, and that Moses' People needed to be prepared to accept the Ten Commandments in a relatively short time.

Shortly after attending this class, I made my one and only trip to Israel, and was part of a 3-person tour. We had a dedicated car and driver, and after spending a night in northern Israel, we were driven south through the Golan Heights. We passed a beautiful village beside a lake, and our driver commented that the lake contained the only fresh water in Israel that isn't owned by the Israelis. He told us that the water belonged to the Druze, and that they were perhaps the only Arabs fully trusted by the Israelis as members of the Israeli Defense Force (IDF). He said the Druze are a very mystical people, and then shared a comment that I find most incredible, "Their Prophet is Yitro, Moses' father-in-law." Perhaps a better understanding of Yitro's advice to Moses is available—embedded in the lore of that beautiful village.

In part my interest in all this came from studying the mystics, being particularly drawn to the Australian aboriginal culture and idea that nomadic peoples find abundance in what appears, through my Western lens, to be a barren wasteland. Their connection to the land and all life, living in mutuality with it, creates an understanding that the Earth will provide as long as it is fully respected. I strongly suspect that Jitro, as the leader of a nomadic people in the wilderness, shared their sense of abundance.

In April of 2012 I had the pleasure of hosting Larry Merculieff, an elder of the Aleut Nation, and told him about my intrigue with the Hebrew language as described by Suares, including the passage regarding Moses and Yitro. He told me that many elders believe that the most fundamental shift in humankind's relationship with the Earth occurred 5-6 thousand years ago. September 2013 marks the beginning of the Jewish year 5774, on a calendar that is said to have started with Moses.

I later learned that in the portion of the Torah that tells of Moses' interaction with Yitro, there is a paragraph that begins and ends with an upside down Hebrew letter-number *Noun*. It's the only place in the Torah where upside-down characters are written. According to Suares, *Noun* is Existential Universal Life. Writing it upside-down suggests it has been negated, lost. Is this the point in time where the Jewish people lost this most crucial Indigenous understanding of our planet?

Batya Podos was also interested in Yitro's advice to Moses, and I asked her if she would explore the Torah portion further. Here is Batya's interpretation and story.

Batya's Interpretation of Yitro and his Role

Prologue

Imagine you were enslaved and now you are free. What story do you tell? If you are a Jew, it's a story about miracles and wonders, revelation and law, and forty years journeying in the wilderness. It's about a land promised, lost, and eventually found. It takes up four of the five Books of Moses, which make up the sacred text of Torah. It is THE story, and we tell it again and again.

From *Sh'mot* (Exodus) to *D'varim* (Deuteronomy), we are reminded to "remember what G*d did for you when He brought you out of Egypt." When we receive revelation at Sinai and the

Divine appears to the multitudes, it is with a voice that says, "I am the Lord your G*d who brought you out of Egypt." It is our bond. We are never to forget what was done for us. It is repeated in liturgy, read in sacred text, and the entire holiday of *Pesach* (Passover) is devoted to telling the story. We are a nation of storytellers, but this is the one to which we continue to return.

Yet it is not the liberation from Egypt that informs our relationship to the Divine and each other. It is what happened afterwards, at Sinai and in the Wilderness.

Yitro

One way to understand this more deeply is to look to the relationship between Moses and Yitro, Moses' father-in-law, Priest of Midian, who is a catalyst for events that have a profound effect upon Moses and the Hebrew people.

We first meet him early in Exodus, after Moses flees to Midian from Egypt for fear of consequences for killing an Egyptian. We are told then that Yitro has seven daughters, that Moses drives off the shepherds who terrorize the girls at the well, and that he is taken in by Yitro, eventually marrying one of his daughters, Zipporah, with whom he has two sons.

At this point, Yitro is called Reuel. This may mean that one of these names is a title or honorific rather than a proper name, or it may be, as is common in Torah, that he is known by several names. However, after this one episode, the name Reuel is only used once again.

According to the energetic patterns set out by Saures for the Hebrew letters, the name Reuel contains the essence of the archetypical, the existential and the cosmic. Looking at the letters that make up the name, we go from *resh*, the cosmic container to *Lammed* which takes the infinite and transforms it into the particular. The name Reuel contains the vision of opening to possibilities, the essential cosmic energy of the universe, and the ability to shape that energy. So here is someone who understands the primal patterns of creation and is able to translate those patterns into contained, focused vision. This is someone who walks in equilibrium between worlds.

Lammed	Aleph	Vav	Ayn	Raysh
30	1	6	70	200

The name Yitro begins with a *Yud*, the smallest and one of the most potent of Hebrew letters, the first letter in the tetragrammaton, the encoded four letter G*d-name. It represents full expansion, a partner to the primal energy of the universe. The *Tav* that follows it represents the complete cycle of cosmic existence, the receptacle or tabernacle of life, held in the cosmic container/cosmic mind of *Resh* and ending with *Vav* which is connection, union and fertilization.

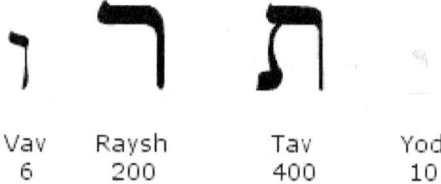

Vav	Raysh	Tav	Yod
6	200	400	10

Yitro, as his name implies, understands the cycle of life in all its levels, from the physical to the metaphysical. He is a conduit for higher energies, yet he is connected and in balance with the physical world and his environment. He is, after all, a Priest of Midian, and is introduced to us as a tribal leader and shaman of the highest degree. And without his interactions with Moses, and his profound effect upon his son-in-law, the story of the Hebrew people would be decidedly different.

When Moses flees Egypt, he is giving up his life of wealth and privilege as an Egyptian prince. He has recognized that he is a part of the Hebrew people enslaved by Pharaoh, yet he cannot live among them. He is at a crossroads in his life, neither the prince nor the prophet he will become.

There is a *midrash*, a story that interprets and illuminates events in Torah, which says that the first thing Yitro did upon meeting Moses was to throw him into a pit for forty (40) days. This was the beginning of Moses' initiation. Yitro becomes his teacher, his guide into the mysteries. Without that initiation, Moses would never have been prepared to receive revelation from the burning bush. It is Yitro, the one who balances the eternal and the temporal, who teaches him.

Once Moses has received his mission and has agreed to return to Egypt, he must ask Yitro for permission to leave. For years he has been living the life of a shepherd, learning the ways of the Midianites, the indigenous people of the region. He has been the apprentice of the High Priest, learning to work in the higher planes, and to keep the physical and metaphysical in balance. Until he met the G*d-force in the burning bush, he may have imagined he had found his place, his life's purpose. But Moses is intended for greater things, and Yitro has prepared him for them. He leaves Midian with his father-in-law's blessing and returns to Egypt to free his people.

The next time we see Yitro is in the *parasha* (chapter) of Torah that bears his name, and it is significant that a Midianite should have a chapter in a series of books designed to establish the formation of the Jewish people. In this chapter, Yitro arrives at Mt. Sinai. Torah says, "Yitro heard all that G*d had done for the Israelites and brought Moses' wife Zipporah and her two sons... to Moses in the wilderness at Mt. Sinai." When Moses sees Yitro, he bows down to him and kisses him, demonstrating the deep respect of student to teacher. This is his prime relationship—we never hear how he greets his wife and sons.

Torah says Yitro "rejoiced, blessed G*d, and offered sacrifices to G*d." Many of the rabbis see this blessing and sacrifice as Yitro's conversion to Judaism. I think that that is not the story. Yitro was Moses' teacher. He prepared the way for Moses to receive revelation, opened the path for him to become a great prophet and leader of his people. Without Yitro's guidance, Moses may not have even recognized a profound moment was upon him when he encountered the burning bush. He may never have established a relationship with the Divine that was more intimate, more transcendent, than is experienced by any other person in Torah.

Yitro, as the Hebrew letters of his name imply, sees and experiences the world through cosmic mind and is utterly connected to everything. He is "plugged in" to the energy of the universe, to the balance of the planet, and to the place of equilibrium between them. He already knows this G*d. He already has a relationship with this Divine Essence. And since he already recognizes that all spirit is One, there is no conflict between his role as High Priest of Midian and the G*d who has revealed Itself to the Hebrew people from the mountain.

Immediately after this, Yitro observes Moses being overwhelmed with people coming to him to instruct them and to settle their difficulties. He tells Moses, "The thing you are doing is not right. You will wear yourself out." He then helps Moses set up a judiciary system which stands as the model for our own legal systems in the 21st century. And when this is done, he leaves and returns to Midian.

When we last meet Yitro, it is over a year later and he returns to Sinai. *B'nai Israel*, the children of Israel, are at last ready to pack up their camp and move into the land promised them—a short journey away. Now the name given him is Hobab, son of Reuel. Some scholars say that this is not Yitro, but his son; others indicate that it is indeed Yitro returned. As mentioned before, it's not unusual for people to have more than one name in Torah. Scholars say Yitro has as many as seven names.

The name Hobab, broken down into its Hebrew letters as set out by Suares, *Hayt, Bayt* and *Bayt*, means undifferentiated, unstructured energy that is held by the cosmic container—which is quite different energetically from his previous names. I believe it indicates a change in his relationship to Moses and the Hebrew people.

And here is the reason I think this is so. To get there, we need to reveal more of the story. Moses asks Yitro to come with them. He tells him that he will be rewarded with a portion of the land that has been promised. But Yitro says no, he will return to

Midian, to his own land and people. Moses begs him once more. "Please do not leave us," he says, "inasmuch as you know where we should camp in the wilderness and can be our guide." Any bounty we receive, he says, shall be yours. We do not know Yitro's reply to this, but we never read of him again.

Immediately after Yitro leaves, the camp sets out. They are prepared. They have received revelation, met G*d on the mountain, received the "ten utterances" and all the law, built and sanctified the tabernacle, ordained priests. They have organized the tribes to march out in precise order to the blasts of silver trumpets. G*d inhabits the tabernacle and is ready to lead them out in a pillar of Divine smoke. They are not at war, not hungry or exhausted from travel. They have, in fact, everything they need to enter the land they've been promised.

B'midbar: lost in a wilderness[22]

And then something happens. In the text, we come upon two inverted *Noun*s. These inverted letters act as brackets for the prayer Moses sings as the tabernacle moves out to guide the people to their destination. The first part of this prayer is still sung today when the Torah is taken out of the ark. It is an invocation: "Arise You G*d! May Your enemies be scattered and may Your foes flee before you." When the tabernacle halts, Moses sings: "Return You G*d! You who are the tens of thousands of thousands of Israel."

According to Suares, the *Noun*s that appear before and after these invocations relate to existential life. In Suares' Kabbalistic system, the *noun* is in the dead center of the *Aleph-Bet* (Hebrew alphabet). It fertilizes the whole, joining inner and outer life in one being. Even its spelling ends at its beginning.

However, there is another definition of the word "existential" and it is characterized by a sense of disorientation and confusion in the face of a world that cannot be understood. This

---

[22] This is the title of this section of Torah, and the name of the days it is read in synagogue. It's usually translated as "in the wilderness" and Batya is using it to refer to the psychological state of being lost, out of touch, disconnected.

is not a state usually experienced by indigenous people. Instead of being in balance with the land, moving in harmony with the energetic forces of the environment and listening for the wisdom that comes from the equilibrium between the spiritual and the physical, existentialism causes a disconnect. The *Nouns* are inverted right after Yitro's presence is no longer among the He-Hebrew people, and this changes their meaning. Instead of flying on the wings of revelation and the covenant, the intimacy with the G*d-connection at Sinai, the balance between the inner and outer, the spiritual and the temporal, there is a loss of faith. And that is exactly what happens once Yitro's presence is no longer among the Hebrew people. Instead of flying on the wings of revelation and the covenant, the intimacy with the G*d-connection at Sinai, there is existential questioning and a loss of faith.

And this happens just as everything is ready to go, not far from reaching the place of promise. Lacking nothing, still the people begin to have strong cravings. Their dissatisfaction spreads and soon there is weeping and crying for meat. The rabbis say that these longings, these cravings, were not just for meat—this is an existential undifferentiated longing, a deep dissatisfaction and overwhelming desire—and this was the unforgivable thing. For with that desire, those cravings, they lost their belief in and connection with the Divine. They lost their link with the energy of the land and the G*d force in everything which Yitro had imparted to Moses.

And in that moment, everything changed. The forward motion, the flow with Divine energy, was reversed and the story of the Hebrew people became quite different from what it could have been. Instead of crossing into that land of promise, there are forty years of wandering, a generation dying, and a new generation learning what had been forgotten.

Unbalanced therefore Unfulfilled

So now we return to this undifferentiated, unstructured energy that Hobab/Yitro embodies in his last visit to Moses. With the double letter *Bayt/Vayt*, he brings a dual energy to the camp, energy that is both resisted and accepted. The *Bayt/Vayt* is also the container that separates that which is held from that which is not. It seems to me that Yitro has recognized a shift in the energy of the Hebrew people. He has anticipated that they will not be able to hold on to a higher state of being and will succumb to their cravings; that they will lose faith. As Hobab, he has both embodied and contained this energy, yet in the end, he must release it to Moses and leave his student to carry the weight alone.

If one believes that Torah is a living document, as I do, not simply something that happened to the ancestors with little connection to modern life, then this is a potent teaching. And it is one with which we still struggle. If we are able to embrace the flow of the G*d-field, to hold the balance, as Yitro does, between the spiritual and the temporal, then we are able to reach our Promised Land—whatever meaning that has for us. But if we are attracted to the superficial, if we follow our desires, our cravings, we are disconnected from our higher selves. Reb Zalman Schachter-Shalomi translates this as, "Don't let your cravings become your gods." In our 21st century American world, where the birth of Jesus is marked by shopping days, and "reality" shows that glamorize greed and bad behavior are on every television channel, we can begin to understand how much work we have to do to disassociated ourselves from our cravings.

Yitro lives at the Source. As a holy man of the indigenous Midianites, he has a special relationship not just with spirit but with his environment, the land upon which he walks. That is one reason Moses wants him to come on the journey. Yitro knows where the water is.

And so does Miriam, Moses' sister. As long as she lives, there is water. She, like Yitro, is connected to the earth and knows its mysteries. We can imagine that she has passed this knowledge onto other women, but Moses doesn't ask any of them to be his companion in the wilderness. He asks Yitro. What the Hebrew women knew and what knowledge they could have shared remains in the white spaces between the letters, waiting to be revealed. It is significant that when Miriam dies, several chapters after this incident, the water—the primary source of life in the wilderness--dries up.

All of this is saying that, when the Hebrew people lost their higher consciousness at the moment of their cravings, they also separated themselves from the wisdom of their inner selves that might cause them to walk on the land in a different way.

After Yitro leaves, between inverted *noun*s, Moses invokes G*d to scatter enemies and foes. But where are these enemies? The Amalekites, the great enemy of *b'nai Israel*, were defeated and there has been no attack, no war. Why was he preparing for war?

Consider this: if all the tribes of Israel, and the mixed multitudes traveling with them, had gone forward as containers of the highest cosmic energy, instead of succumbing to their existential yearnings, when other nations encountered them, they might have recognized the G*d-field within them, and there might never have been the need to conquer.

At the beginning of this chapter I wrote that this is a story about a land promised, lost, and eventually found. Promised in covenant and revelation, lost in the inability to stay connected to the higher self/G*d-field, and found by the end of Torah, after forty years of re-learning and re-connecting to what had been lost, when *b'nai Israel* is finally ready to cross the River Jordan.

Yet, I think, the promise was never complete because in the end we crossed the river as conquerors rather than as a people who embodied the balance of cosmic forces, who truly were, as Torah exhorts the Hebrew people to be—whole/holy, a nation of priests and priestesses.

Staying Connected

So we continue to return to the text, to the vibrancy of the Hebrew letters which are set out as maps and markers to lead us on the path, and we strive to repair our deepest selves and the world. The lesson of Yitro is to stay connected, to be in dance with the whole and not be distracted by the insubstantial.

I believe that if we keep this in front of us, we can retell the story of the wilderness. We can then fulfill our ancestors' promise of wholeness and balance, and heal the past as we heal the present.

Milt's Perspective on Yitro

Before ending this chapter, there are two other points I'd like to add. The first is that Suares writes about "the most ancient of ancient traditions (the Qabala)" and states,

> Frequently, over the centuries, the Qabala has been lost and rediscovered.... Looking backwards in time, we can see that the Qabala was alive with Mosheh (Moses); going back further, we find it with Abram; in still more remote ages, it disappears from the sight of enquirers, but not from the perception of those who have inherited that most ancient of ancient knowledge.... The source of the original Qabala can, however, be grasped at any time, because it is timeless.[23]

Suares then writes how the Qabala was smuggled out of Egypt,

> ...to save it from the Egyptians, and gave it in trust in Median to descendents of Abraham.
>
> The mythical Reuel is clearly said to be (according to his name) Elohim's shepherd. Informed by his symbolic 7 daughters about the man who "delivered" them, he understands that, after so many years of waiting, he that was to be the inheritor of the Qabala has at last come."[24]

So Suares is clearly of the opinion that Yitro (also called Reuel) is the messenger who imparts the ancient wisdom of the Qabala to Moses, with the possibility that it would be grasped by the Israelites before they went to Mt. Sinai and the Promised Land.

My second point is that, with Batya, I believe the upside-down '*nouns*', signify the loss of understanding of 'Existential Universal Life'—the attraction, oneness, and connectedness of all life among its components and with its Creator. This leads to the receiving of the Ten Commandments, which was an incredible social contract, very necessary in its time, but insufficient for experiencing the harmony and connection that is essential for a balanced, sustainable life. It therefore led to severe consequences for humanity, because for millennia very influential cultures have

---

[23] Suares, ibid, p. 19.
[24] Ibid. p. 31.

focused on them and so failed to internalize the concepts and guiding principles of Universal Life.

"Hidden" Patterns & Possibilities

Ruth L. Miller

Prologue

Growing up in a family whose years in India before I was born were a part of our daily life, with an aunt who'd married into Judaism and converted, and being surrounded by Christians of various sorts, the relationship between the various languages and theologies was a constant source of intrigue and wonder. Learning the words "Shalom," "Salaam," and "Shanti-Om" in totally different environments, then suddenly realizing they all meant the same thing was one of my great "wake-up calls" as a girl. And one of the transformative moments of my life came when, while caring for my Jewish cousins on a Friday evening I really heard the words being said as they blessed the bread and wine for Sabbath, then 2 days later, attending my first English-language Catholic mass, being nearly overwhelmed by the realization that precisely the same words were being said!

Over the following years, as a student of anthropology and of religions, I would come up against just such moments again and again. And it continued through my attempts to make sense of the shift from Neolithic, goddess-oriented garden cultures to urban patriarchy, from the "Noble Savage" of what were still called "primitive" cultures to the barbaric behaviors of so-called "civilized" cultures.

I came to see finally that there is a clear pattern and process when I realized that the place to look is not in the scholarly records and writings, but in the brief references buried in them and in other works that describe life as it was truly being lived. I discovered that, while the traditional scholasticism and the actual descriptions are often in direct contradiction, frequently the information needed to resolve the apparent difference is right in front of anyone who "has eyes to see."

Mrym's Story

As an example, as Batya has pointed out, in, around, and between the stories of Moses and Yitro is another story; that of the woman named Miriam.

We first meet Miriam when she is appointed by her mother to guard the basket in which the infant Moses has been set adrift. Then it is Miriam who meets with Pharaoh's daughter and convinces her that taking the child will not be a problem and, then, to have Moses' biological mother act as a wet nurse for the baby!

We don't hear about her again until the actual Exodus.

And then, what a role! Aaron, Moses, and Miriam—together leading their people out of bondage; together comforting the fearful. And then, when they are safely across and the waters have rushed in to destroy the soldiers chasing them, it is Miriam who leads the celebratory dance! The Hebrew people clearly look up to her at this point, and follow her leadership.

On the trail, though, things change. Initially, she is part of the council with Aaron and Moses—until Moses' non-Hebrew wife enters the picture and Miriam dares to ask Moses why he would marry a woman from outside the tribes.

That's the turning point in her life. That's when her name, which has two roots, one "proud," "tall," "regal," and the other "bitter," "resentful," shifts from the former meaning to the latter. Its root also includes the word myrrh, the sacred substance used to anoint kings and to heal the sick.

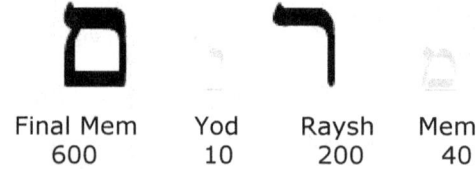

Final Mem	Yod	Raysh	Mem
600	10	200	40

Again, we see that *Mem*, on both ends of the word, with *Raysh* between them. The Cosmological comes into the existential and with it the transformative energy between Existential Birth and Cosmic Fertilization. It's a powerful name, rich in meaning.

Now, from the point of view of the cultures around the Hebrews at the time, it would make perfect sense for Miriam to assume one of 2 things. On the one hand her brother would take the daughter of one of his most important tribal leaders as a wife, to bind the tribe's allegiance—perhaps keeping his Midianite/Cushite wife as a "second" or concubine, not unlike what Abraham, Jacob, and others had done before him. Or, given that they'd just spent several hundred years in Egypt, where the Pharaoh consisted of a brother/sister-husband/wife pair, Miriam may actually have thought her brother would take her for his partner-wife so they would lead their people together.

However, as the story unfolds, not only Moses, but G*d Himself is angry with Miriam for even thinking that Moses should marry anyone else. She is turned white, like a leper, and then thrown out of the community to live with the other undesirables for a week. Finally, she is miraculously restored and returns to the community. And we do not hear of her again, except in some of the *midrashes*, which tell us she knows where the water is, as Batya alluded to in her story of Yitro, above.

Then, many years later, we're told by one of the prophets that she died on the journey and that a well, a spring, was named after her. We never hear anyone given the name Miriam again, not anywhere in Torah nor in the other books of the Hebrew Bible—not even in the Apocrypha.

The closest we come is when it's time for Naomi to take over as Headwoman of Bethlehem, arranging for her adopted daughter Ruth to marry Boas, the Headman—and she announces to the community that her name is now "Mara", from the same root.

The next time we find the name is in the New Testament, when Yeshua ben Yusef, called *Yezu* in Aramaic and *Jesu* in Greek, is followed and supported by not 1, but 6(!) Miriams (in Greek, Mariamne—in English, Mary), including his mother and the Magdalene—from 6 different places, all of whom are wealthy, independent women who can choose to travel with a wandering rabbi and make sure his needs are met. They are also the ones who remain present at the foot of the cross.[25]

Clearly something remarkable has happened, in all these stories. Some process and pattern is being demonstrated.

Weeping for Tammuz

Another pattern to be found in the Hebrew scripture is even more deeply buried.

From about 3000 years B.C.E., long before *Torah* was written, there were stories written in Sumeria about a powerful deity named Inanna, who had a lover named Tammuz, and whose jealous sister, queen of the Underworld, arranged for Tammuz to be killed and taken to her realm below the Earth. As the story goes, Inanna was overwhelmed with grief and went to all her relatives to find out what she could do. Then, following their guidance, and covered with the 7 principles of divinity in the form of veils, she went down into the Underworld. There, at each stopping point, she gives up one of those seven layers of protection, finally ending up at her sister's throne totally naked and vulnerable. She persuades her sister to allow Tammuz to return to life with her and, 3 days following her descent into hell, she returns with her resurrected beloved and they are immortalized as the crescent moon embracing the evening star.

Throughout the history of the region and still, today, the dance of the 7 veils re-enacts this powerful story. In the Book of Jeremiah, written about 700 years B.C.E., the prophet complains that the "women still weep for Tammuz" and in the New Testament, we learn that Salome (a Greek version of the Hebrew word *Shalom*) performed the dance before her stepfather, the king. The names have been changed over time and across regions, but the dance and its implications remain.

Scholars studying the pre-empire cultures of the Middle East attribute the story to the annual reenactment of the birth, death, and resurrection of a plant, its seeds, and its harvest. Tammuz is the seed; Inanna the life force that goes into the Underworld to

---

[25] For more information on the role of the Marys, particularly the Magdalene, in Jesus' life, see my book *Mary's Power*.

bring new life to the apparently inert seed; the budding plant then is the resurrected Tammuz.

The dance re-enacts a story that has been all but forgotten. But it, too, is a form of language: using movement instead of sound to communicate an ancient idea in a way that all who see it can comprehend—and at the deepest, nonverbal level.

The story, and the dance that conveys it, reminds us of a hidden pattern and process that, when we see it, helps us understand our ancient heritage and current life—and opens up new possibilities for the future.

The Pattern in the Stories

If we look deeply into these two stories—the Miriams and Tammuz—what we see is that underneath and behind the written, codified history of the Hebrew culture another history has been happening. And if we look at the cultures in the area at the time, we see that they're part of a larger pattern. We realize that the Miriams in the New Testament are direct descendents of Moses' sister: They are the Wise Women, the headwomen of their villages and tribes, and they have continued, through dance and story and practice of the healing arts, to maintain their connection with the cosmological and archetypal processes that Suares and Milt are pointing us to, today.

Finding the Possibilities in the Patterns

Because the Western mind has been shaped by the Indo-European language structure—and particularly, in recent centuries, its written form—we're not attuned to seeing and hearing the power in the words we use and the stories we tell. In fact, we rarely even pick up on their clear meaning. For example, the word "inspiration" has the same root as "respiration" and "expiration" but we're so used to thinking of them in their usual contexts that we don't realize they all have to do with both "spirit" and "breath." "Aspiration" is in the same family, so our usual definition of it as "hope" goes beyond to "movement from spirit" and "having breathed."

Similarly, Westerners, when we read any work of literature, tend to read it literally, forgetting to look for deeper meaning and possibilities. When we do so, the whole story, the whole world, becomes an unfolding metaphor. For example, to go up onto the mountain may be read as to raise one's consciousness or lift one's aspirations, while to descend into darkness is seen as falling into sadness, grief, fear, and anger. And to open a door is to have more possibilities available, while to close a door or a path is to become more limited. To be carried by the river or currents is to "go with the flow" and a tempest is emotional as well as physical. From this perspective, every encounter is information: to see a hawk or eagle, or rabbit or mouse, tells us something about where we are in the moment.[26] Almost every action and experience becomes an opening to deeper understanding.

Nor do Westerners realize that the part of us that governs our life processes accepts everything we say as what is true for us—and as what we intend. So to tell ourselves and others, over and over, that we "need a break," or are "too fat" or "can't get enough (whatever)," or are "broke" is to say it to ourselves as if we are commanding ourselves to be that way.[27] Seeing the world and our language this way helps us to realize the power of our words. And as we do that, we begin to choose them very carefully.

Also, the stories we tell ourselves, and read and watch in books and movies, and listen to from the people around us, all contribute to the Patterns and Possibilities of our lives. As I suggested earlier, the Indo-European language tends to focus on an action being done by someone to something or someone. So our stories focus on that process—and aim to be ever more exciting and intense. Other language groups, not focused on action but on relating, tell stories of deepening relationships or understandings. In those cultures, it's not possible to be a victim or a perpetrator, so they don't have them in their stories—or in their lives. This is part of why Indo-Europeans have been able to pretty much take what they want from their Indigenous neighbors—there's no lan-

---

[26] Ted Andrews' *Animal Speak* and the Sama' *Medicine Cards* are useful guides for this way of experiencing such encounters.
[27] This is the essence of Ernest Holmes' work, *Science of Mind*.

guage, no story in those cultures that allows for behaviors that we assume to be "normal."

Is it possible to find a new pattern? A new way of thinking that leads to new possibilities? We believe so.

PART 3

LIFE

"Now, fortunately, the other side of human consciousness can come into play. We can use our consciousness to reconnect with the wisdom of nature. The Latin term for 'reconnect' is *religare*, the origin of the word 'religion', so religious awareness in its most profound sense is this reconnection with the wisdom of nature, which we can and must actualize." ~ *Fritjof Capra*[28]

---

[28] "Psychotherapy - Insights Into Interconnectedness" by Swati Chopra: "An interview with Dr Fritjof Capra, physicist and internationally reputed author of the tao of physics, during his recent visit to India" on www.lifepositive.com

The Story We Live

"Thus conceived, the dialogic mind is not only a guardian of liberty but metaphorically similar to a democratic state. It rejects the tyranny of a single system or dogma; it welcomes new ideas and guarantees them equality as it considers them; it provides an open forum for competing theories and systems; it refuses to censor "dangerous" ideas; it cherishes and protects its capacity to learn and grow; it guards as something precious its own access to joy and laughter." ~ *Robert Grudin*[29]

Milt Markewitz

Prologue

Greg Braden writes the following in his Introduction to the *Cipher of Genesis*:

> Does not the sacred thus humanized fall under Jesus' curse: 'Get thee behind me Satan: thou art an offence to me: for thou savourest not the things that be of God, but those of men?'[30]

My understanding of this is that only goodness emanates from Creation, that the essence of all life is pure, and that impurities have been introduced by humans. In this context, there is only one type of suffering, that imposed by humans. What we consider to be suffering based on acts of Nature, and we call 'natural disasters' are seen as the planet re-establishing balance and harmony. And the grief we all feel when something we love is lost can also be understood as a deep appreciation for whatever or whoever was loved.

How do we 'savourest the things that be of God'?

My first suggestion, that we pursue understanding the Hebrew language as articulated by Suares, is the focus of the first part of this book.

---

[29] *On Dialogue*, Robert Grudin, p.5
[30] Suares, Carlos, *The Cipher of Genesis: The Original Code of the Qabala*, p. 11

My second suggestion is that we follow Suares' assumption that Hebrew was one of many languages that emerged from, and maintained, an understanding of the energies of the planet and local connectivity, and listen to those peoples who have maintained the integrity of their language.

I suggest we start with our Creation Stories.

Creation

We've already explored the Hebrew story, but there are as many such stories as there are cultures on the planet.

In Thomas King's *The Truth About Stories*, he tells us a Native American creation story followed by his interpretation of the King James Version of "Adam and Eve," the Judeo-Christian creation story. And when he's done he compares the two renditions:

> A theologian might argue that these two creation stories are essentially the same. Each tells about the creation of the world and the appearance of human beings. But a storyteller would tell you that these two stories are quite different, for whether you read the Bible as sacred text or secular metaphor, the elements in Genesis create a particular universe governed by a series of hierarchies–God, man, animals, plants–that celebrate law, order, and good government, while in our Native story, the universe is governed by a series of co-operations–Charm, the Twins, animals, humans–that celebrate equality and balance.[31]

My Jewish upbringing has led me to the understanding that we are very much out of touch with our cosmology. We may read Genesis occasionally, but the story reflected in our prayers and our psyche, is the Exodus story. Our ethics lead us to focus on social order rather than ecological integrity. This isn't surprising when we discern the basis of our ethics as the Ten Commandments and realize that they are essentially a social contract. They tell us who we should be in relationship with one another in the present moment, while being sustainable requires that we have a strong ethic regarding both:

---

[31] Thomas King, *The Truth About Stories*, pp. 23-4.

1. Who we are for the Earth, and
2. Who we are for future generations.

I think it is also fair to say that not only are the Creation stories different because of who is telling them, but they are received in vastly different ways based on the language spoken by the listener.

These different ways may be expressed in terms of cultural norms and consciousness. They can be better understood when mapped into 'Archetypes for Sustainability' listed in the very first graphic, in the Introduction to this book:

From these archetypes we can articulate the paradigm shifts necessary for us to be a sustainable society, and the associated learning that must take place. And at the heart of the learning is an appreciation for language that enhances our relationships with all life.

Understanding what 'The Binding of Isaac' was intended to convey is of critical importance because in some ways the current understanding gives all who accept it a license to sacrifice their children. This may sound paranoid, but how do we explain our behavior of trashing the planet when somewhere inside we all know that it is the future generations who will pay for our neglect? We're already seeing disastrous effects of global climate change as small islands and coastal areas are being decimated by rising oceans. Throughout the planet we're seeing mass extinctions, negative impacts on growing food, and devastating weather patterns. Compounding all this is that often the technological solutions are developed by the same consciousness that caused the problems, and simply exacerbate the problems.

Changing the Story

Changing our religious stories can be excruciatingly difficult since they represent our current 'truth', and we defend them in sometimes violent, punishing ways. But sometimes changing a deeply held story can surface and overcome the dissonance that the story created.

Let me share a very powerful interfaith experience that was the culmination of some profound interfaith relationship building.

Good Friday

After Rabbi Aryeh passed away in 2009, we asked a protégé of his, Rabbi David Zaslow, who leads a synagogue in Ashland, Oregon if he would provide us with Rabbinic services one weekend a month. One of Rabbi David's activities was to lead an interfaith class based on a book he'd written, *Roots and Branches: A Sourcebook for Understanding the Jewish Roots of Christianity, Replacement Theology, and Anti-Semitism.*

One of the participants was Pastor Barbara Campbell, whose St. Mark Presbyterian Church is where the P'nai Or congregation holds its services, classes and many religious and social events. Rabbi David and Pastor Barbara became fast friends.

On Wednesday evening prior to Good Friday of 2011 the St. Mark choir was practicing, and when they saw the P'nai Or person setting up for Jewish Friday night Shabbat services, they realized there was a potentially difficult problem to work out— they had committed the Sanctuary to P'nai Or on the evening that they were planning to hold Good Friday services. Rabbi David was coming up the next day to lead a class and services, and Pastor Barbara decided that she would wait and make a decision with him. They wrestled very hard with their options for either divvying up the space, or finding what we might do together. They decided to have a joint Good Friday service in which they would begin with the lighting of the Shabbat candles, and then have the Jewish participants serve in Witness to the Good Friday service. Pastor Barbara felt compelled to change the 'Passion Story' so that the Jews wouldn't be blamed for Jesus' death. Rabbi David was on the pulpit with Pastor Barbara during the entire service, and when it came time to bless the bread and the wine, he chanted the Hebrew prayers. Together they hosted a joint Communion, and when the Good Friday candles were extinguished, the Jewish participants witnessed the St. Mark folks leaving the Sanctuary in silence, then followed in silence.

We had been tenants at St. Mark for seven years and became close in many ways, but never had we bonded as we did that evening. As I hugged St. Mark friends, I had the profound feeling that having the Passion Story retold was critical in lifting the barriers, perhaps subconscious, which had kept P'nai Or from being fully accepted by our St. Mark hosts.

I do quite a bit of Interfaith work, and view that particular Good Friday service as more than an event. It's a process through which every once in a while there is an expression of love or courage that makes us fully human and transcends the dogma that defines so much of our stories.

Guiding Principles

Several years ago I was on the board of the Spiritual City Forum of Portland. Our monthly lunch meetings featured a speaker, followed by a brief time for questions intended to stimulate dialogue, then a dialogue at each table. Our program theme was to better understand the sustainability teachings of various religions. I invited a Jewish colleague who was studying Environmental Sciences, Shamu Fenvyesi, who I thought 'walked his talk' both as a Jew and a steward of the Earth.

He agreed to share and spoke eloquently of Jewish Law, the commandments, our covenant with God, and some of the scriptures related to our relationship with the Earth. He shared a Jewish story intended to alter our thinking by touching our emotional and spiritual core. And he spoke of Jewish ethics: our belief in 'original goodness' and the notion that there are constant, ongoing, ethical breakdowns that must constantly be repaired; how it is our responsibility to perform virtuous acts toward humankind and the Earth; and how it is a gift to perform these acts because they are all part of a virtuous cycle.

Shamu's talk was wonderfully received and the questions that were asked by participants to stimulate the dialogue that would follow reflected people's appreciation. Then, as the question period came to a close, a gentleman in the back of the room asked, "How do you reconcile your humanitarian way of being with Israelis shooting Palestinians in their olive groves?" An uncomfortable silence followed his question as we proceeded into the small group dialogue portion of our program.

When the luncheon was over, I asked the gentleman who had asked the difficult question if we could have coffee together, and we set up a date. As the time approached, feeling I had to organize my thoughts well and in a non-argumentative way, I decided to see if I could develop a construct based on guiding principles that can stimulate a generative conversation.

The graphic that follows, 'Archetypes of Religion', is based on the assumption that every religion has, to one degree or another, four basic guiding principles. The graphic may be misleading in that each principle is drawn as a concentric circle, when, in fact, the degree to which one principle or another exists varies in each religion, but it worked for the purpose at hand.

In this graphic, the 'pie' represents any and all faiths, with each 'slice' being one faith tradition. And there can be a slice for those who claim no faith at all. Each concentric circle encompasses a part of each slice, and represents a guiding principle that, as stated above, I believe exists to one degree or another in each faith tradition.

The gentleman I was meeting with, John Nichols, brought his wife Caroline with him. They are of the Baha'i faith. We explored the chart and each of us quickly concluded that Shamu,

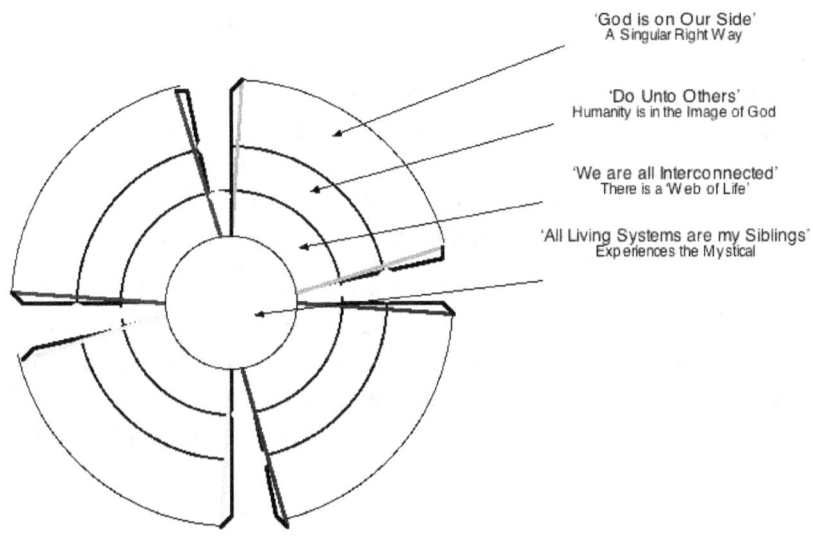

the speaker at Spiritual City Forum, was coming from the circle at the center of the drawing, his primary guiding principle being 'All Living Systems are my Siblings.' The Israelis shooting at Palestinians in their olive grove probably believed a literal interpretation of the Old Testament and thought that God had bestowed all of what is now the State of Israel to the Jewish people for all time, and that therefore 'God was on his side.' What followed was truly a generative conversation, and I remain very good friends with both John and Caroline.

I have used this chart on many other occasions as a way of stimulating Interfaith understanding and dialogue. Often the conversation reveals the belief that the outer circle has embedded in it a world view of 'scarcity', win/lose, no sharing, while the inner circle has embedded in it a sense of 'abundance'—infinite in terms of love and blessings, embracing all life, and with humanitarian behavior being paramount when it comes to social justice.

Also, it seems that each of us usually operates around more than one of the principles: one that we predominantly claim and a second that often strongly influences our primary principle.

The two guiding principles in the middle are perceived quite differently depending on how they are influenced by the outer and inner principles. 'Do Unto Others,' if most strongly influenced by the inner circle, elicits virtuous behavior, but if the influence is the outer circle it becomes 'an eye for an eye'. 'We are all interconnected' is somewhat the same. Given our language with its subject-object structure, from an outer circle perspective we perceive ourselves as a 'collection of objects,' but with an inner circle perspective we become 'a communion of subjects.'

There are people who live from the center of the pie outward, whom I call the mystics. They energetically connect with the Universe and have generated a love for all life so that our essential humanness supersedes any religious dogma, and the game of life, as they play it, is based around guiding principles rather than rules.

Games of Life

The notion that all of life can be lived as one of two types of games, one with a rules base called 'finite', or one based on guiding principles, called 'infinite', is clearly articulated in James Carse's book, *Finite and Infinite Games; A Vision of Life as Play and Possibility*. Examples of related finite and infinite games abound. For instance in the legal field, litigation is a finite game, and justice an infinite game; in athletics, winning games is finite, while sportsmanship is infinite; and in education, training is finite, while learning is infinite.

One of Carse's most profound observations about the nature of these two types of games is that a multitude of finite games can be, and usually are, played within the infinite game, but the infinite game can never be played within a finite game. If this is true, it would seem axiomatic that you can't play the infinite game of 'global community' or 'diplomacy' under the finite game of 'the war on terror, ' but you can play 'the war on terror' under the infinite game of 'global community.' When you think about it, it's probably the only way the 'war on terror' can be won.

Our perception that we must play either the finite game of being a superpower, or the infinite game of being part of a new world order needs to be changed so we can be playing both simultaneously.

A question that I pondered when I read Carse's book was, "What creates 'lose/lose' situations?" In the examples cited above, participating in athletic events without a sense of sportsmanship, or entering into litigation without a sense of justice, creates lose/lose scenarios. This realization led me to suspect 'lose/lose' occurs when we are playing finite, 'win/lose'- games without understanding the necessity of being governed by guiding principles, making it so that no 'win/win' situation exists.

This is also what we're dealing with when we grapple with becoming sustainable. We are playing win/lose games in every facet of our lives without adhering to guiding principles of social and ecological order. These guidelines serve as an ethical compass and when we get 'off course', we may experience serious consequences. Our tendency has been to label the consequences of our own actions as problems to be solved, and the very framing of our work in this manner leads to creating more finite games without ever realizing the presence of an infinite container.

Wisdom Consciousness

"In the old days, when a people were gravely threatened, the Chiefs, Medicine people, Shamans, and Elders called Councils. They looked for solutions to their problems by aligning themselves with the ancestors, the natural world and their wisdom traditions. Recognizing that illness is often the consequence of violations of the earth, the community and the spirits, they searched for systemic responses to assure healing." ~ *Deena Metzger*[32]

Milt Markewitz

It's becoming universally recognized that our way of life on Earth is no longer sustainable—that our source of life, this planet Earth, is rapidly becoming overwhelmed to the point where she may no longer be able to sustain us. Many of us have squandered the blessings bestowed upon us for so long that we cannot articulate a clear path to re-achieving sustainable lifestyles.

However, there are many peoples who do articulate what it's like to live in ecological and social harmony. They are very clear regarding when we lost our balanced approach, have developed prophecies that result from unsustainable actions, and told us what must be done to re-achieve balance and harmony. These comprehensive, cohesive stories are told by the Indigenous Peoples everywhere, and when we listen we are compelled to ask, "How do they teach their children so that they understand and practice all that is essential to life and to their culture?"

My answer to the question was largely formulated in December of 2009 when I attended the Parliament of World Religions in Melbourne, Australia, a gathering whose design and content was largely influenced by the Australian aboriginal people. My days were filled with attending sessions facilitated by indigenous educators. I listened for their curricula and instruction

---

[32] Deena Metzger, April 2008 letter, Mandlovu/Topanga Daré ReVisioning Medicine Council

methodologies, as well as where their work might have been co-opted or contaminated by Western educational ways.

When I returned to my home in Portland, Oregon, I enrolled at Portland State University (PSU) and began taking courses in Native American Studies. I learned more about both the atrocities that had been perpetrated against the First Nations, and the spiritual underpinnings of life for these oppressed peoples.

In one class I constructed the "Pedagogical Comparison" chart, below.

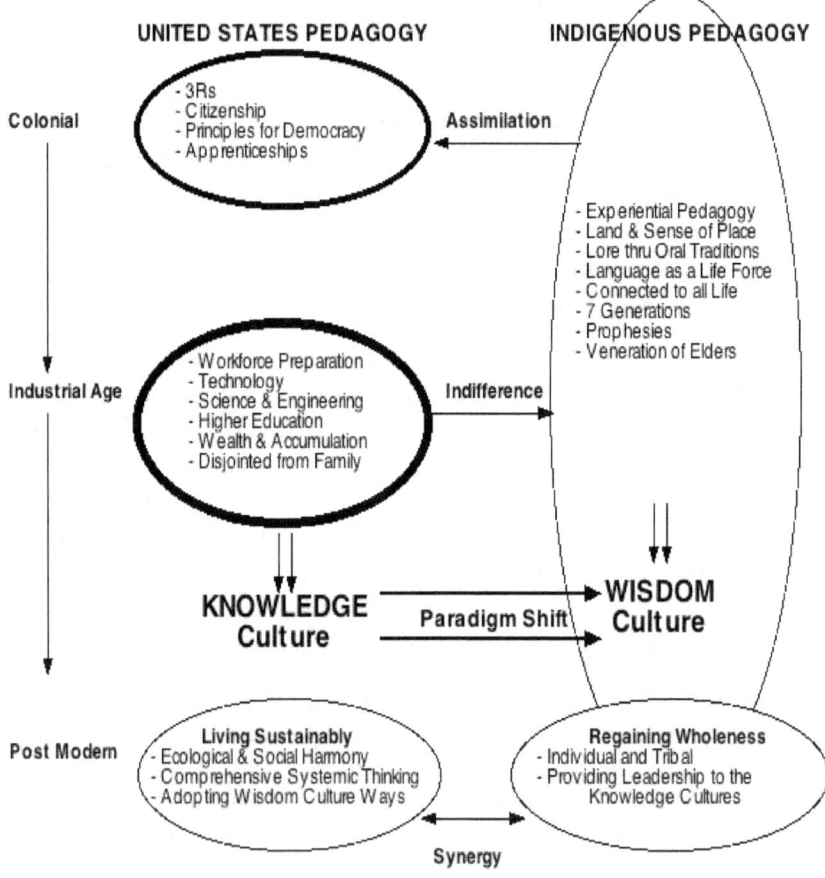

It shows:

> How curricula have changed dramatically in American public education, yet remains relatively unchanged in Indigenous cultures

- The change in dynamics between the cultures from assimilation in Colonial times to indifference in the Industrial Age
- Our Post-Modern need for understanding Indigenous Wisdom as a key for re-achieving Global sustainability.

After a Native American mentor, Mr. Terry Cross, saw the 'Pedagogical Comparison' chart he said: "Milt, wisdom for me is knowledge that's understood relationally." I think this is a most succinct expression of 'Systemic Understanding'.

This chart and other work I did at PSU caught the eye of Dr. Cornel Pewewardy, Director of Indigenous Studies, and he asked if I would work with him to design and facilitate a workshop for teaching First Nations' children who were being educated in public school systems. I agreed and moved forward assuming that we wanted to blend the Western 'knowledge'-based education with the Native 'wisdom'-culture approach.

Spiritual Ecology

While doing that work, I referred to the following work by Dr. Gregory Cajete, and when I better understood how Native cultures are grounded in 'Spiritual Ecology', I changed my assumption away from blending Western with Native pedagogies and toward the question: "What is the basic pedagogy that underlies Indigenous Cultures?"

Dr. Gregory Cajete, in his book, *Look to the Mountain: An Ecology of Indigenous Education*, describes a process that he calls "The Ebb and Flow of Tribal Education." As he presents it, the whole process is grounded in Spiritual Ecology, "For Indigenous People, Nature and all it contains formed the parameters of the school" and is informed by two very complex, dynamic processes. His first set of processes consists of:

- Mythic,
- Visionary, and
- Artistic.

These are designed to "develop a deep understanding of the inner being." His second set,

- o Environmental,
- o Affective and
- o Communal,

are "the outward, highly interactive, and external dimension of Tribal education."[33]

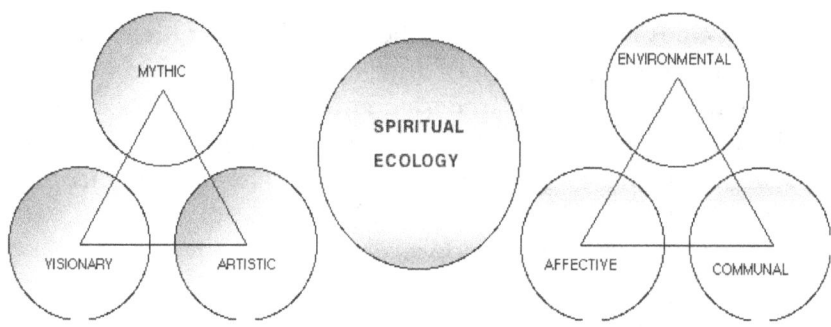

In all this there is a sense of timelessness, an understanding that the cherished virtues, ethics, and guiding principles of the ancestors are the basis of our desired future for the generations that follow, and we must live these virtues every day in order for them to become our reality.

With Spiritual Ecology as the heart of Indigenous education, Nature becomes the mentor and model that is understood in terms of processes and relationships, balance and harmony. Earth becomes *our* steward (in direct contradiction with the Judeo-Christian model), where the relationships are mutual and co-creative. The primary thought process is organic rather than mechanical, and the worldview is one of limited abundance where the Earth's capacities to renew, cleanse and heal are always honored.

---

[33] Gregory Cajete, *Look to the Mountain: An Ecology of Indigenous Education* p. 39.

Memes

The term Spiritual Ecology resonated deeply for me, and it struck me that some very similar terminology was utilized in Don Beck's *Spiral Dynamics*.

The essence of *Spiral Dynamics* is that every culture operates out of one or more 'memes' or mental models of who we are, individually and collectively, in terms of our values, basic worldview and level of consciousness. As individuals and as a culture, we evolve (or devolve) in a spiral from one meme to another—always including some of what we've learned and practiced from previous memes.

The list below describes what people in each meme seek from life, that is, their goals for whatever they call 'successful living'. The upward spiral progresses in the order of the list shown below—the lowest meme, using the least of our human potential, being Beige and the highest, maximizing our potential as spiritual, intellectual, and physical beings, Turquoise.[34] The current meme can be said to be the current consciousness of a culture.

> BEIGE, 1st stage of human development/experience: survival; biogenic needs satisfaction; reproduction
>
> PURPLE, 2nd stage: safety/security; protection from harm; family bonds
>
> RED, 3rd stage: power/action; asserting self to dominate others; control
>
> BLUE, 4th stage: stability/order; obedience to earn later reward; meaning
>
> ORANGE, 5th stage: opportunity/success; competing to achieve results; influence
>
> GREEN, 6th stage: harmony/love; joining together for mutual growth; awareness
>
> YELLOW, 7th stage: independence/self-worth; fitting a living system; knowing
>
> TURQUOISE, 8th stage: global community/life force; survival of Earth; consciousness

---

[34] From the website: http://www.spiraldynamics.org/Graves/colors.htm

Memes & Wisdom

I've found this idea of memes as used in Spiral Dynamics to be very informative. For example, in 2003, shortly after we began the Iraq War, I was in a workshop where a 15-20 minute Spiral Dynamics overview was presented. Prior to the war, I would have characterized the United States as being in the Stages 4 & 5, the Blue and Orange Memes, stuck a little in 'Stability & Order' yet pushing very hard for 'Opportunity & Success.' The Progressives in the culture seemed in a struggle to move the country up to the 'egalitarian, communal' 6th Stage, the Green Meme. But when the war began with its 'Shock & Awe" tactics, I felt the U.S. spiraling downward into a warring, authoritarian, 3rd Stage, the Red Meme.

In listening to and reading about Indigenous pedagogy, I feel that Cajete and others are describing an 8th-Stage culture, the Turquoise Meme. This is particularly ironic since such peoples have typically and wrongly been described by colonizing cultures as primitive and/or savage, which would be attributes of Stages 1 & 2, the Beige and Purple Memes.

It's clear to me, and I hope to the reader, that there is a very different consciousness being demonstrated between the prototypical Western memes, even the ideal memes in Western culture, and the idealized Indigenous meme. In fact, when we talk about ecological sustainability, I think it's fair to say that Western consciousness created our sustainability dilemma and the Indigenous consciousness offers the solution.

Understanding this, it became clear to me that it is extremely important that we *not* blend education approaches or impose cultural ways that compromise the indigenous ideal. Instead, we must learn to listen and accept the leadership of the indigenous people who embody some or all of this ideal. It is their wisdom, based in Spiritual Ecology—being in balance and harmony with the Earth and all life—that can guide all of us to create relational social structures and sufficiency lifestyles that are economically and ecologically sustainable.

Wisdom, Language & Memes

The wisdom embedded in Spiritual Ecology isn't new—it hasn't been only available in the last 30 years, as stated by Don Beck and too many others—but has been a part of indigenous cultures for tens, even hundreds, of thousands of years.

In fact, when Indigenous peoples from diverse geographical locations are brought together, we find that they're able to connect deeply almost immediately as they share their stories, customs, songs, dances and food, and that there is a common, agreed-upon, earth-based, wisdom to which they mutually adhere.

An example is documented in a video, *Yakoana*, that shows how, in a 10-day gathering prior to the 1992 Rio de Janeiro UN Conference on Development and the Environment, nearly a thousand tribal leaders from every continent developed extraordinary relationships through the sharing of their cultures and rituals built on the common concern for Mother Earth. From the deep trust and love that was created, and the sharing of the deepest of guiding principles for life, there emerged a Manifesto.

You see, the Indigenous peoples of the world were given only 5 minutes on the conference agenda, and their spokesman, Marcus Terena, a Native South American, organized this First World Conference of Indigenous Peoples to give them an opportunity to share in those minutes. The Manifesto they composed was essentially what he shared during his limited time.

For me, it is absolutely astounding that peoples with no common verbal or written language and from diverse cultures from all around the world could come together for such a short time and come up with a consensus on how to address the most significant challenge humanity has ever faced.

A conclusion that I draw from all this is that lower memes vary in terms of their ability to connect with higher memes, and the path for individuals, and thus cultures, to shift upward is highly dependent on their language. To the degree that the peoples of lower memes experience revelation through language, they connect individually and as cultures only through various print and electronic media. People of higher-meme cultures, on the other hand, experience revelation directly, feel in their hearts their connection with all life and how it works, and develop a spiritual basis for their lives. Sacred Ecology is, therefore, the essence of the Turquoise meme.

A corollary to this is that a particular language may make it much more difficult to progress from a lower to a higher meme. I suspect that English, particularly the way it is spoken in America, where the thought process is based primarily on reductionism and the world-view is one of scarcity, makes it difficult for us to move as a nation into the Yellow and Turquoise memes. Suares' commentary is:

> ...the words we use in our languages are conventional. They do not emanate from the objects which they designate. The word house is understood just as well as *maison* in French or *casa* in Italian: none of those words has any ontological link with the essence of the object thus specified, and their use merely helps us to recognize such objects, by means of linguistic agreements.[35]

His conclusion when speaking of ancient Hebrew texts is as follows:

> ... the decoding of Genesis and of any other cabalistic text is therefore not a mere matter of transposing from A-B-C to Aleph-Bayt-Ghimel, but a process of penetrating an unknown world by means of a manner of thinking which has to be experienced by the very language which must be learned in order to understand it. However paradoxical and perhaps difficult this may appear, it stands to reason that were Revelation a matter of ordinary words, it would be an obvious fact prone to superficial observation.[36]

---

[35] Suares, Carlos, *The Cipher of Genesis: The Original Code of the Qabala.* pp 13-14.
[36] ibid., p. 14.

Honoring Differences

"...seeing knowledge and knowledge creation as the cornerstone of what makes an organization successful...
...seeing all organizations as embedded in, and interdependent with, larger natural and social systems...
...How work is organized must be guided by principles of living systems...
Together, these three elements could be the basis for a second industrial revolution that would close the circle and enable humans to live once again as part of, rather than apart from, nature." ~ *Peter Senge*[37]

Milt Markewitz

Prologue

As children most of us learn that whatever we're experiencing on a day-to-day basis is "normal" and anything else is "different," "weird," or "odd." Part of becoming a mature human being is opening to other ways of thinking and experiencing, which then helps us to clarify our own values and vision.

The Power of the Human Dynamics Model

I shared the 'Pedagogical Comparison' chart from the previous chapter with Dr. Vivek Shandas at Portland State University, and he asked me if I could articulate the essential differences between the 'Knowledge' and 'Wisdom' cultures. I told him that the best work I knew of to explain the differences was the study of 'Human Dynamics' by Dr. Sandra Seagal. Dr. Seagal developed her understanding by following her intuition that people's voices resonated for her in different parts of her body – some in her chest, others around her mouth, and a third higher in her head. She would invite small groups who resonated in one area or the other to her home to cook a meal together, and after they'd eaten, share what was important to them in conversation. What she

---

[37] Foreword to H. Thomas Johnson & Anders Broms' *Profit Beyond Measure: Extraordinary Results through Attention to Work & People*

found was that the groups representing each area were distinctly different, and that multiple groups who resonated within her in the same area were very similar.

Seagal concluded that human beings are born with one of three preferences (Physical, Emotional, or Mental) for how we take in information and another one of three preferences (also labeled (Physical, Emotional, or Mental) for how we process it. She labeled these preferences 'Dynamics.'

THREE UNIVERSAL PRINCIPLES:

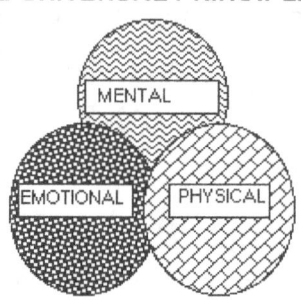

EACH OF US HAS ONE OF THREE PREFERRED WAYS OF BRINGING IN INFORMATION (FILTER) AND ONE OF THREE PREFERRED WAYS TO PROCESS.

IT IS THE COMBINATION OF PROCESS-FILTER THAT DEFINES EACH PERSON'S DYNAMIC.
Example -- A person whose process is PHYSICAL with an EMOTIONAL filter is referred to as PHYSICAL-EMOTIONAL

Thus, there are 9 possible Human Dynamics emanating from this 3x3 construct, and it turns out only 5 are found in any significant number in any known culture.

Cultural Differences

As she went around the world teaching her theory and helping people identify their own dynamic, she collected data. The data shows that the percentages of the dynamics from one culture to another vary widely.

WESTERN DYNAMICS

85% Process

EMOTIONALLY

1/3 Mental (about ideas)

2/3 Physical (immediate connections)

INDIGENOUS DYNAMICS

Approximately the same % Process

PHYSICALLY

A small fraction are Mental

A large fraction are Emotional -- energetically connected with life

The chart shows that in Western cultures about 85% of the population process *emotionally:* 1/3 of these are Emotional about their ideas, and the other 2/3 Emotional about their immediate feelings. On the other hand, indigenous and many Eastern cultures have a very high percentage that process *physically.* And, where Western cultures tend to be oriented on the individual, Indigenous peoples tend to focus on the group.

Few people are surprised by these differences, yet we don't try to explain them, and some mistakenly conclude that some ways of processing are inherently better than others. The fact is that each dynamic has its strengths and weaknesses, and we all need to appreciate each type of processing and learn how to integrate them, both internally as individuals and collectively in groups.

Individual Differences

It should be noted that while bringing together people of the same dynamic allows us to see the stark differences among dynamics, the most significant power of Human Dynamics is in integrating the dynamics within each individual, and combining strengths when each person in the group is aware of their own and everyone else's dynamic. This integration process helps us to fully understand systems, develop comprehensive solutions to our most difficult problems, and recognize that learning begins very differently for each dynamic.

One of the major contributions of Human Dynamics is the recognition that learning begins very differently for each dynamic. The predominant dynamic in Indigenous cultures is Physical-Emotional, that is, they bring in data to which they are deeply connected (Emotional) and process it systemically (Physical). By contrast, the predominant dynamic in Western schools is Mental-Emotional. Here are some quotes from the Human Dynamics website addressing the consequences of this situation:

> In schools in the United States, Canada, Sweden, and Israel where we've worked, we've found 50 to 60 percent of the children identified as having learning problems to be physical-emotional, though they represent only 5 to 10 percent of the population. Often they're labeled "slow learners." To date,

we've found few of these children to be actually learning disabled.

Generally speaking, physical-emotional individuals need two crucial elements: physical involvement in the learning process and time for individual exploration, absorption, and digestion. To help the physical-emotional learner, educators need to present extremely clear instructions, preferably presented as a series of steps. These learners must understand the practical purpose and utility of the material and how they will be expected to use it.[38]

Orientation:	Individual (I, me, mine)	Group (we, us, our)
Time:	Present & Immediate Future	Continuity of past, present into the long term future
Learning:	Linked to individual experiences and interpretations. Requires experiment & self expression.	Through detailed texts; hands-on experiences; in organic time; through repetition
Movement:	Spontaneous	Deliberate
Communication:	Expressive of individual personality, ideas, feelings, and subjective awareness.	Factual; detailed; expressive of group decision-making.

It's readily accepted by most people that Indigenous and Eastern cultures think more holistically in that they're more inclusive, consider generational consequences, and have an intuitive understanding of being in harmony with the Earth. Also, among educators there's an acceptance that our schools don't seem to understand where learning begins for most indigenous students.

Sandra Seagal and her husband David Horne videotaped triads of young students put together by their dynamic build model parks. The differences among dynamics are clear in terms of how they reacted to each other, related to the materials, what they produced, and how they viewed their work. As a professor who saw a video of the children building the parks commented,

I've just seen five beautiful works of art (the park models), none of which I could assess accurately if I didn't know the

---

[38] http://www.humandynamics.com/index.php/implications-for-education?start=1

student's dynamic, and none of which I could judge fairly if I didn't know my own dynamic.

Our challenge is clear when we recognize that virtually no one knows either their own dynamic or the dynamic of others, and to the degree that we don't, we have neither accuracy nor fairness in our assessments.

I find it amazing how few people know about Human Dynamics and why it isn't more widely utilized. I'm left with the following questions and responses:

- Why isn't this study widely used?
    - Quite probably because the colonized cultures don't trust the colonizers to accept that each dynamic is equal in that it brings unique valued, necessary perspectives to bear.
- Might Human Dynamics be accepted as a useful tool in Indigenous Pedagogy?
    - Quite probably 'yes' because Indigenous peoples tend to be more inclusive and holistic, and will understand that all perspectives are necessary for addressing concerns.
- In addition to the mental and emotional intelligences that are so widely recognized in Western culture, might there also be a physical intelligence?
    - I think the answer is quite clearly 'yes' and is exhibited wherever there is mutuality with Nature and all life forms.

When we begin to accept that life can be experienced in different ways with equal validity, then we begin to be open to a whole new level of life and learning.

Honoring Ceremony as Transformation

In October of 2011 I had the honor of attending a American Indian Institute, "Hear the Ancient Voices" gathering, hosted by the Iroquois and Mohawk People 40 miles west of Albany, New York. There were 50+ non-Native people and approximately 20

Native American leaders. The former were asked to listen and learn, and go forth with the messages that resonated with us.

Ms. Vickie Downey, a Tewa elder from Tesuque Pueblo, shared with us of a gathering in early October of 2010 when Indigenous peoples from North & South America met in Albuquerque, NM to share prophesies. Several of the prophesies told of the need for Native Americans to reconcile among themselves and with the White people in North America as a prerequisite for attaining sustainability on our planet. Mr. Jake Swamp, Faithkeeper of the Mohawk nation Tekaronianeken, who I had the honor of meeting at the Parliament of World Religions in 2009, articulated a vision to bring about reconciliation in North America. Jake's daughter accompanied him to Albuquerque, and realizing that he was very sick, escorted him home before the gathering ended. Sadly, Jake passed away just days later.

Vickie then shared with us Jake's vision and the commitment that she and several other tribal leaders held to make it a reality. The plan was to reconcile through ceremony by having Indigenous peoples come together for several days over the Summer Solstice of 2012. As Vickie was finishing her talk we were joined by two Native women who were embraced warmly by each of the Native people in our group. They were introduced as Jake's daughter and his widow, Judy.

After lunch that day Judy was sitting by herself and I was drawn by her strong, quiet presence. I asked if I could sit with her for a few moments, and she was very gracious. I expressed my condolences, and mentioned that I had met Jake at the Parliament the year before and we had exchanged emails afterward. She shared with me that this was the first time she had been in public since his death, and how she appreciated what we were doing at this gathering and her opportunity to speak. I was deeply touched.

Vickie would keep us abreast of details, and what we subsequently learned was that representatives of the Tribes from Canada and the Eastern US would travel from the east, and the Tribes from South America and the Western US would travel from the west to gather for 5 days over the summer Solstice, from June 18-23, at the headwaters of the Mississippi River in Minnesota.

When I shared what I had learned there with colleagues in Portland, we decided that we would do what we could to help raise money, awareness, and frequent flier miles to support the Summer Solstice ceremony. Ms. Irene O'Conner, of the New Thought Center for Spiritual Living in Lake Oswego, Oregon, organized two services—one on June 18th and the other on June 23rd, so that we might share in spirit with our Native brothers and sisters during their convocation.

Bringing about transformation through ceremony was quite foreign to me, as I believe it is to most of us in the Western world. I'd always found ceremony to be largely symbolic, providing comfort through traditional ritual. During this time I thought about the ceremonies where I had experienced transformation. They were rare, and never of the magnitude of the Summer Solstice Ceremony. So I asked Elders who I thought might enlighten me and read a couple books and several articles, and the conclusions were always the same. First, ceremony is absolutely integral for life-cycle and other transformations for many cultures, and second, I would have to experience it in a new and profound way before I could ever say, "I'm beginning to understand."

Sun Dance

This summer, 2013, I was invited to attend a Sun Dance. I want to be very careful what I write, as I believe the Sun Dance to be very sacred, and I was a guest who only scratched the surface regarding what was to be learned. I was very honored, and profoundly changed.

I arrived at the Sun Dance site the day before the dancing would begin in order to attend an organizing and information-sharing meeting. When I arrived I could see a very large number of tents and tepees grouped around what appeared to be common cooking and gathering, canvas covered, arbors. I asked one of the security people who checked me in how many people were expected, and he told me over 400. I was amazed, and assumed we would have quite a long meeting. The meeting started at 3pm and covered all that we would need to know about protocols, food, costs, ice deliveries, porta-potties, security, the moon lodge, and I can't remember all the other topics. For each topic, someone stood up from the audience and gave a succinct talk on what we needed to know. Often there were concerns like not enough money to cover the costs of the 8 meals to be served in the communal kitchen, and needing signup for security, etc., and in each case it was assumed that everyone would pitch in to provide whatever support was necessary.

The meeting was over before 4:30. I was stunned, and knew that I was part of something very special. It seemed to me that there wasn't a need to dwell on problems because there was a mutual trust in a community who would address any and all issues once they were surfaced.

I left after the meeting to go to stay with my daughter's family for the evening and pick up a tent and other supplies that I would need. So I missed the selection and mounting of the sacred tree that would stand at the center of dance arbor, and serve as the focal point for prayers and strength for the dancers.

When I returned, I set up my tent among folks that I mostly new from the Earth & Spirit Council of Portland. I met some new people, learned more of what to expect, and turned in early, as wake-up would be around 5:15am for supporting the Opening Procession at 6:00am.

The Sun Dance lasts for 4 days and the Dancers are both men and women who go without food and water in what turned out to be very hot weather—a couple of days over 100 degrees. Each day there was an Opening Procession, followed by four dance rounds, and a Closing Procession. The dancing was held in a large, open, circular area surrounded by an arbor where the hundreds of supporters could stand and sit, with a place for the Dancers to rest between rounds at one side. There appeared to be a single dance step repeated over and over again, and there were several men and women to support the Dancers.

I learned that the Dancers are dancing more for their people than they are for themselves, and this is why it is so important to be present and support them each time they dance. Male Dancers are tethered to the tree through inserts in their chests. Some break free in the round they are tethered, and some, the Eagle Dancers, are tethered for each round, each day.

What I experienced outside the dance arbor was every bit as informative regarding community and ceremony. Everyone seemed to operate according to guiding principles of helping, sharing, and addressing whatever needs arose. I was helped to understand what to expect and what was expected of me. There was an air of genuine friendliness and caring. I wasn't quite family, but the invitation was there. One of the things I was most impressed with was the openness and trust: the local cooking and gathering area with all their food and equipment were wide open, and each of the tents and tepees seemed very accessible, while honoring others' privacy. When I mentioned my observations to a colleague, he stated that in a previous year there had been a thief who was caught, and he was embraced by the community in such a way that he was welcome at this year's Dance.

One of the things that I was most taken with among the Dancers was the compassionate support they received from and provided others throughout. As you can imagine in such a physically and emotionally exhausting endeavor, many of the Dancers broke down and wept. They were compassionately led to the tree and cared for until they were ready to resume. There seemed to be a guiding principle of keeping everyone within the community of Dancers, and most of them recovered relatively quickly, while others sat out a round or more before participating again.

In addition to the 'Prayer Rounds' of the Dance, there were several rounds that seemed life changing for the participants, and deeply affected me.

The first was a Veteran's Round in which both men and women who had served in the military were honored. It was apparent that many of them had carried home deep physical and psychological wounds, and the round was intended for healing. There were emotional breakdowns, and the support from the Dancers and fellow veterans never wavered. I saw many of the veterans after the honoring, and spoke with a couple. It was clear that they had had a transformative experience.

The second was a Children's Round, and many of the children were accompanied by Sun Dance participants. The pride of the parents and the children was palpable. I should also mention that children accompanied by parents or grandparents were included in a round each day.

There was another transformative moment that I'd like to share. It occurred on the 4th day. A Native elder living in Portland, Rod McAfee, who has dealt with severe health challenges for the last three years, joined us. He was sitting in the front row for a morning round when one of the Dancers, who had at one time been incarcerated, asked to come see Rod. The Dancer was escorted to where Rod was sitting and thanked Rod for "Saving his life." I knew that Rod had worked in the prisons, and assume he had counseled this young man, perhaps run a sweat in the prison. Rod doesn't hear well these days, and when his wife Linda told him what the Dancer had said, he asked him to come back. The Dancer was escorted back. Rod talked to him for several minutes, and then he was escorted back to the dancer's rest area. I don't think there was a dry eye anywhere. Rod's work in the prison, the Sun Dance, and now Rod's presence in this ceremony all seemed to converge into a moment that Rod, with his wisdom, solidified a life-change for this young man.

Closure for me was complete when in the last dance round the Eagle Dancers, surrounded by their community and supported by all the other Dancers, broke from their tether. I don't think I can express the incredible pride that emanated from the community. This was followed by the Procession of the Dancers so that we could each see each other in a very close and personal salute to all that had transpired.

I had a choice to stay another evening and participate in the next day's feast and give-away or to say my goodbyes, break camp and head for home. I chose the latter because I felt as if I had experienced transformation in a profound way, and I wanted time to reflect. Also, I didn't feel as if I was quite yet 'family' with these wonderful hosts, and perceived the feast and give-away to be 'family' events.

I came away with the realization that transformation through ceremony is the norm in many cultures. What I learned through experiencing it is how very real it is, and that it is accessible to all of us if we just want to incorporate it for completing life-cycle events and invoking necessary life changes.

In addition, my Sun Dance experience gave me hope. Unfortunately, the U.S. government banned these Native ceremonies from the late 1800s until quite recently. The Sun Dance that I attended is less than 20 years old, but already we are seeing the positive effects, as children who attended the first Sun Dances are now coming of age and marrying, having children, and participating both in the community and as Dancers. I spoke with several people who've struggled in Western society, but found a path for themselves through such ceremonies that's grounded in an appreciation and gratitude for life, ecological integrity, family, and community. By learning from others, and intention on our own part, I believe that any of us who wish to can participate in and shape a desired culture based on our most cherished virtues.

The Indigenous Way of Thinking

I think it's very important to reflect on cultures that through their language understand life processes and know at the deepest level the sacredness of the social and ecological systems they are participating in. They understand their personal and collective responsibility to maintain balance and harmony, and recognize it as the basis for ecological sustainability, as well as social wellness and economic viability. These are the Wisdom cultures.

Two of the primary mental attributes of such cultures are that their thinking is very organic, and their worldview is one of abundance, with limits. They are organic in that they appreciate all life, connect with it deeply, and express it artistically and in every other facet of their culture. Their sense of abundance is limited because it emanates from a knowing that the Earth provides as long as we accept the responsibilities of a mutual stewardship. These two attributes might be considered the basis for their understanding of Sacred Ecology, for their living lives in balance and harmony, and for their spiritual practices.

Indigenous and Western worldviews

They also serve as a starting point for understanding Western paradigms, as well as overcoming the duality trap that is so easy to fall into when we do these comparisons. When the above framework is shown graphically it's easy to place the characteristics attributed to indigenous peoples as one end of a duality, and to show how the other end of the duality helps us define Western Culture. A part of this graph might look like this:

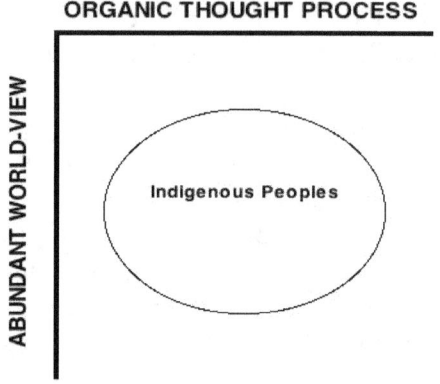

The idea for this graph came from Dr. Tom Gladwin of University of Michigan in a 'Systems Thinking for Sustainability' workshop in Portland in the mid-1990s. The last exercise in the workshop was to take a quiz that Dr. Gladwin used to collect data whenever he presented to business groups or sustainability oriented folks like us. The quiz consisted of 40 questions, each with only 2 possible answers, half of which were oriented toward whether our primary thought process was 'Mechanical' or 'Organic', and the other half whether our worldview was of 'Scarcity' or 'Abundance'.

Dr. Gladwin concluded from his data that there are 2 basic Archetypes:

> ➤ 'Sustainability ' folks who are very worried about 'Scarcity' caused by over-population, peak oil, peak soil, potable water, and clean air, and wish to deal with these shortages with compassion (his connotation of 'Organic')

> ➤ 'Business' folks who believe 'Abundance' is infinite and can take what they need, and process it 'Mechanically.'

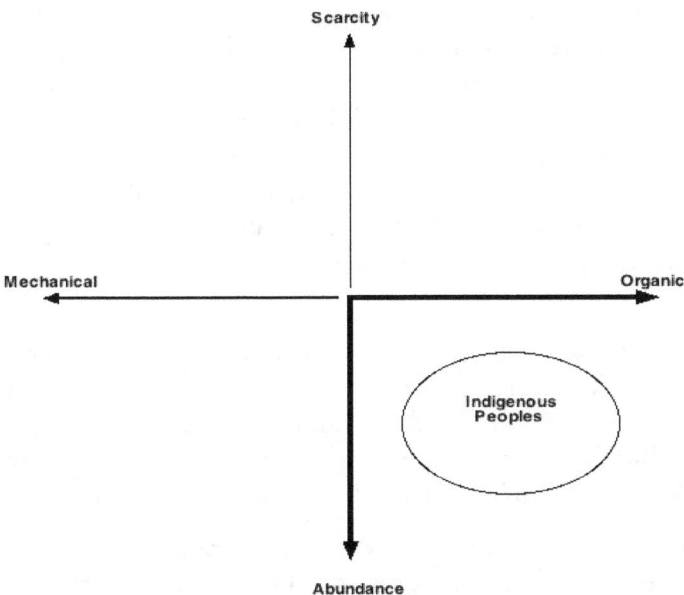

I had quite a bit of dissonance with his conclusions, primarily because I consider myself to be a sustainability person, but I don't think I reside in the upper-right hand quadrant.

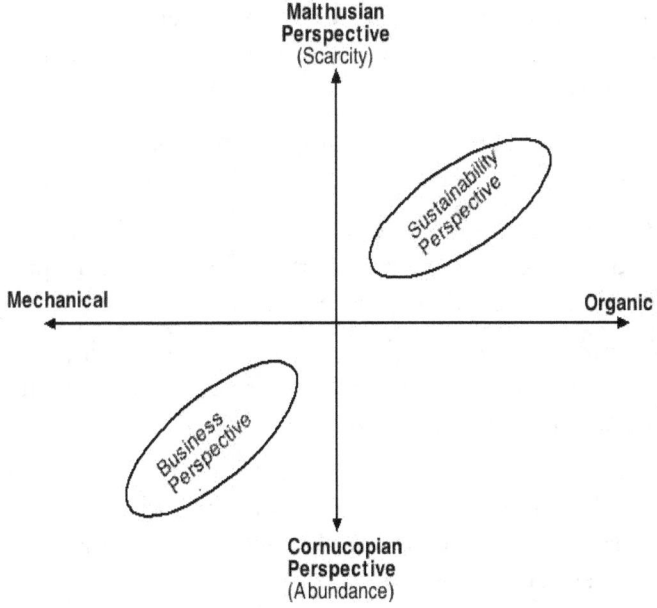

When I saw Dr. Gladwin the next day I asked him if he'd thought about the other two quadrants. He said, 'No, what do you think they are?", and I shared with him that I thought the upper-left hand quadrant was the 'Warring/Colonial' perspective, and the lower-right quadrant the 'Indigenous' perspective. When I shared my 4-quadrant understanding with Dr. Gladwin, I knew I hadn't figured out how to properly name the upper right hand quadrant. It clearly didn't represent the 'Sustainability Perspective'.

As I pondered the subject, attended other Sustainability workshops and conferences, and reflected on how all this fit together, I concluded that this quadrant was best labeled, 'Social Action.' It's the large number of people among us who view sustainability as more of a social justice issue than an ecological one.

Now the concept of social justice is driven by our strongest Western directive, the Ten Commandments, which provide a social contract that guides us to answer the question "Who are we for each other?" But that directive doesn't guide us to ask:

- o "Who are we for the Earth?" and
- o "Who are we for future generations?"

Each of these questions is critical, necessary even, if we are to re-achieve sustainability, but only sufficient when included as the full triad of questions.

This gives us a new, more complete graphic, including the following archetypes:

- ➢ 'Business' is defined by those who believe in the type of abundance that is infinite so they can take and take, and they will process the resources mechanically.
- ➢ 'Warring,' which might also be labeled 'Colonizing,' is defined by those who perceive scarcity and use mechanical force to take and claim ownership.
- ➢ 'Social Action' is defined as those who fear overpopulation, decimation of our planet, pollution of critical resources, and who wish to deal with the resultant scarcity compassionately.

> 'Indigenous' is defined by those who live organically (which is quite different from the 'Social Action' who are driven more by fairness than balance and harmony), and a limited abundance where we take only what we need, take responsibility for ecological well being, and live our lives essentially without waste (which is very different from those who have a sense of dominion and think they can take whatever they perceive they need).

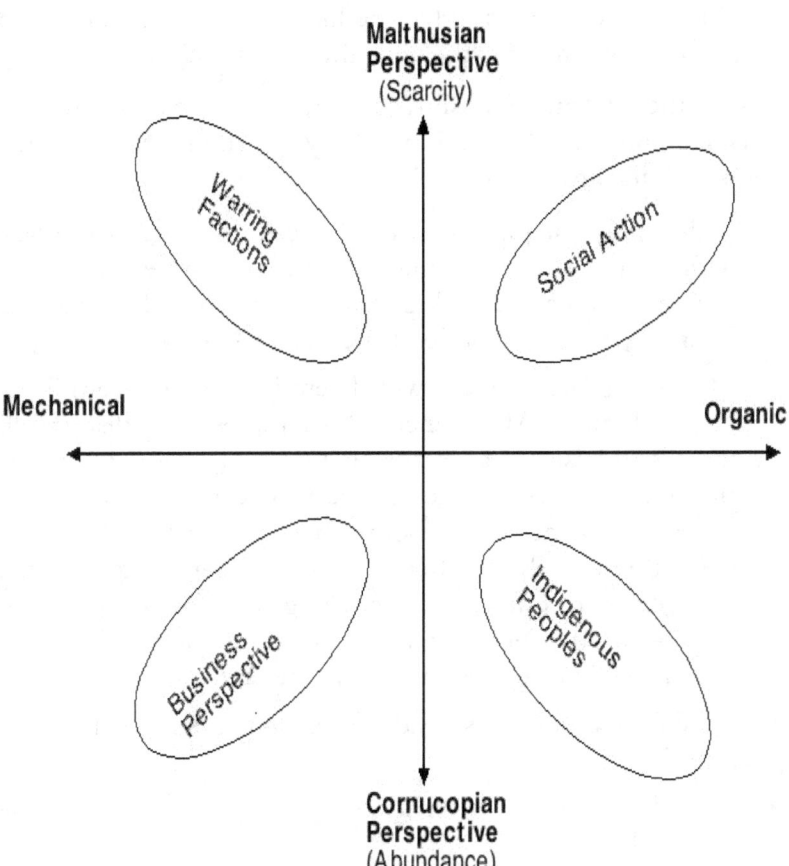

Three Major Paradigm Shifts

Matthew Fox, in a workshop I attended, pointed out that the 3 archetypes 'Business,' 'Warring,' and 'Social Action,' are each segments of our predominantly 'knowledge' culture, and that the 'Indigenous' archetype is predominantly a 'wisdom' culture.

Infusing the knowledge cultures with wisdom so that they also become predominantly wisdom cultures is one of 3 necessary paradigm shifts that this graph shows us, and are the focus of this book. I hope it's becoming clear that there's something much more than just what Indigenous Peoples do that makes their lives sustainable—there's an underlying ethic, a way of thinking and feeling, which governs how they live their lives each day.

The other 2 paradigm shifts are pre-requisites for creating and maintaining a wisdom culture. They are the shifts described by the horizontal and vertical axis:

- Changing our primary science from Newtonian Physics, with its mechanical orientation, to Living Systems, with its organic orientation. (A possible curriculum for teaching Living Systems is described later in the book.)

- Changing our primary worldview from (perceived) Scarcity to (limited) Abundance. This requires us to distinguish what is truly scarce and sharing it, to understand living sufficiency lifestyles, and to reduce procreation. It should be noted that almost all of our current sustainability activities—Reduce, Reuse, Recycle; conserving energy, water, and scarce resources; and creating and following standards—are attempts to take us to a sufficiency life style. The questions we must honestly face are:

- "Will our activities lead to us living sufficiency lifestyles?" and

- "Will sufficiency lifestyles be enough to ultimately be sustainable?"

There's one more stage in the 'Archetype for Sustainability' graphic that I'd like to share, because I think it can be a framework for mapping the flows that have led us to this tragedy of our Global Commons, as well as the flows to overcome our sustainability dilemma.

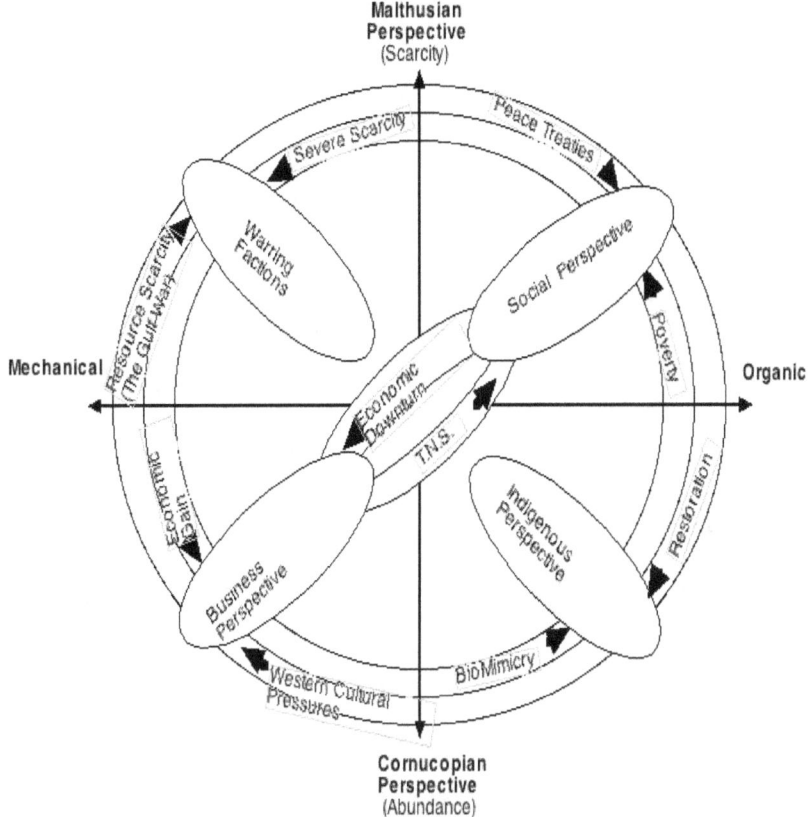

Recognizing that visual art is a language too, my hope is that this graphic might be used as the basis of artistic productions for telling the story in more motivating ways.

Understanding Systems

Ruth L. Miller

In Western culture, as we have seen, the focus is on the individual and what can be acted on, acquired, held onto, and profited by. People in Indigenous cultures, as Milt has so beautifully described, think in a very different way: about themselves, about the Earth, and about their relationship with it.

Is there any way to bridge that gulf? To make that shift?

It's been my good fortune to be a student and teacher in a field that seems to offer a solution.

In the years following World War II a number of people were sure the necessary shift in thinking had begun. The Marshall Plan was in full swing; the United Nations was being born, foreign aid was becoming an assumed part of the budgets of Western, industrialized nations. And, in a conference center in New York City, a few hundred people were gathering to explore how a new way of thinking could be applied within the framework of Western scientific study.

The gatherings were called the Macy's Conferences, having been funded by a branch of the Macy family. Among the people attending were the young but already well-known Margaret Mead and her then-husband, Gregory Bateson. Another couple who would make great names for themselves in their chosen disciplines were Elise and Kenneth Boulding. A young German physicist, Heinz von Foerster, volunteered to prepare the transcripts as a way to learn English, and went on to establish the Biological Computer Laboratory at the University of Illinois. A neurophysiologist from Britain named H. Ross Ashby also attended. As did the two main stars of the series: Ludwig von Bertalanffy, a German biologist whose soon-to-be classic text *General System Theory* had recently been translated into English, and a young American mathematician named Norbert Weiner who'd been conscripted as a "human calculator" during the war, providing coordinates to anti-aircraft gunmen so they would know where to point their guns so the ammunition would actually reach the planes. His book, *Cybernetics,* had just been published and was turning many minds inside out. These are just a few of the better-known scholars who were in attendance.

Over the course of several meetings, these brilliant minds attempted to understand something that was totally unlike anything they were taught in school: the idea that it's the communication between the elements of a plant or animal or society—not the matter or its structure—that determine its behavior and survivability.

Bertalanffy, though a biologist, had developed some mathematical equations to help walk people through the basic concept. He made it clear that no part of any organism could function effectively without the rest of the organism, and that the flows of matter, energy, and information through the whole organism were what kept it going.

Then Weiner, a mathematician who happened to love plants, was able to take the work the next step. He demonstrated how, by following the sun's path in the sky, the sunflowers in his garden were accomplishing everything he had done with a slide rule and radio during the war—they had a built-in control-and-correction system that somehow communicated information to the cells controlling the flow of fluid through the stems, letting which cells know how much fluid to block and how much to allow through so that the petals would constantly face the sun.

The brilliant but eccentric Ashby, with his deep understanding of brain structure and function, took Weiner's equations the next step, basically demonstrating that the control functions normally assigned to the brain must, in fact, be distributed throughout the organism.

This was all the anthropologists, sociologists, and economists present needed to begin to apply these ideas to families, organizations, and societies. They could see, over and over, that it's not possible to understand any individual or group in terms of its physical structure alone. It didn't matter if a company or nation appeared to have a dictator if the actual decision-making was happening at the level of the individual worker. Likewise, it didn't matter if part of a person's brain was not functioning if another part could support the needed information flow. And, if there were alternative routes for producing and distributing goods, the "official" economic structure was irrelevant.

Through the 1950s and '60s, these people explored and experimented with these ideas. Ken Boulding then went on to the Institute for Applied Sciences at Stanford University and created the Society for General Systems Research (now called the International Society for the Systems Sciences.) At annual meetings of the Society, scholars from many disciplines would gather from all over the world to understand this way of thinking and apply it in more areas.

In the late 1960s a Japanese anthropologist named Magoroh Maruyama took these ideas and was able to demonstrate how there is no one controller in any natural system, but a balanced set of increasing and decreasing processes that together lead to the harmonious functioning of the whole. He called them "mutual causal loops" and his work led to a whole new approach to social systems analysis and the design of computer programs to model them.

By the 1970s, the computer had evolved to the point where some of these ideas could be tried out. Jay Forrester created a computer language called Dynamo at the Massachusetts Institute of Technology that allowed him to track how matter, energy, and information might flow throughout the world, as the production and use of food, energy, and basic resources changed. He called this project the "World Model" and folks who used it began to realize that there are limits to the growth of population and resource use on this planet.[39] This is part of what led to the various environmental regulations and organizations that were put in place throughout Western cultures over the next decade.

---

[39] Donella Meadows, Jay Forrester, et al. *The Limits to Growth,* 1972. A Later version, using much more accurate data was published by Meadows in 1994, called *Beyond the Limits.* The modeling language is called Dynamo, based on Fortran—it's also called Stella and is available for a Mac.

At the same time, a new science was emerging that used many of the same principles: ecology. An ecologist looks at the relationships between the different life forms in any given forest, lake, meadow, pond, or other defined combination of plants and animals. In time these began to be called "ecosystems" and the patterns in their ongoing processes began to be understood. C. S. "Buzz" Holling was a major contributor to the process of identifying patterns within the apparent chaos. So "wild nature" began, finally, to make sense to the Western mind.

With that realization and the emergence of a new kind of mathematics and computer programming came the understanding that most of what had been seen as chaotic, unpredictable behaviors in our natural environment were, in their own way, orderly, and to some extent, predictable. Waterfalls and turbulent streams were described in mathematical equations and made visible on computer screens (and later as computer graphic images in movies). Turbulent storms and ocean currents, too. A whole new field of "complex systems" was born, with Chaos Theory, fractals, and fuzzy logic as its underpinnings, and banker-turned-rancher Dee Hock offered the term "chaord" to describe them.

At the same time, that German physicist Heinz von Foerster was visiting Chile, where then-President Allende was seeking to lift his country out of the backwaters of the global economy using some of these ideas. He had Foerster, with Welsh cybernetician Stafford Beer and some others like them, working with some of the brightest minds in the Chilean universities to create a new kind of economic system. Among those were two biologists: Francisco Varela and Humberto Maturana. Together with their mentors these two were able to create a new understanding of how organisms and social organizations form and maintain themselves. They called it "autopoiesis," which is taken from the Greek and means "self-creating." Together, they proved beyond doubt that each and every living system starts as a seed of possibility and draws from its environment the matter and energy it needs to survive and develop to its full potential while maintaining a boundary between itself and its environment.

During those same years a biochemist named Ilya Prigogine was realizing that it isn't possible for most structures to remain the same without a consistent flow of energy—and if that flow stops or changes radically, the structure no longer exists. He called them "dissipative structures," and won a Nobel Prize for the concept. A simple example of his idea is a whirlpool—it only exists if there's water flowing through it. A more complex example is our own bodies—they only survive if there's a consistent flow of matter and energy through them.

And, during the same period, John R Platt, a physicist writing in the U.S. "Bulletin of Atomic Scientists" offered the idea of "hierarchical restructuring.," Drawing on the principles of quantum mechanics, he suggested that at certain points in the life of any organism or organization (including nations), a significant shift in the matter, energy, and information flows might lead to a "quantum leap" from one level of functioning to another. A small group of mutually supportive workers becomes a movement; a monarchy becomes a democratic republic; a cluster of different kinds of cells becomes a new kind of organism.

Another insight from the field of quantum physics was the realization that the observer and the subject being observed are working together as a system—we can never consider ourselves "apart from" whatever we are observing. The data collected in quantum experiments made it clear that there is no separation between us and anything we perceive or measure; therefore the very act of observing or measuring changes the system.

In 1990, an organizational specialist named Peter Senge identified Systems Thinking as "the 5th discipline." In his very popular book by that title, he emphasized the information feedback loops that are the means by which systems maintain themselves or change. And, most important to his method, was the understanding that delays often occur between the action and its felt effect. These delays, he explained, were why managers so often fail to be effective in achieving their desired outcome. They're also why societies often fail to manage their environments.

Over the decades, as these wide-ranging concepts were brought to conferences and published in journals, the fundamentals of systems thinking began to become clear:

- A system is a set of elements interacting together as a whole.
- There is one whole system, the universal system, made up of many elements, with flows of matter, energy, and information sustaining it; everything else we might call a system is a subsystem of that whole.
- Because everything is interconnected through these flows, it's not possible to do any one thing—every action has both immediate and local effects and long-term, long-distance consequences.
- To observe a system is to become part of a new system that includes it and the observer, affecting its behavior.
- Matter, energy, and information are constantly flowing and the balance of these flows is what leads to harmonious function within the whole system and any subsystem within it.
- The flows of matter, energy, and information follow cyclical patterns both within and through a system—increasing and decreasing over time.
- Systems that are open to information flows tend to increase in complexity, are negentropic, while systems that are closed to information or are controlled by outside information systems tend to deteriorate, subject to the laws of entropy.
- Complex systems have multiple subsystems, each with their own pattern of matter, energy, and information flows, and so can appear to be chaotic and without order, but there are always orderly patterns in apparent chaos.
- As organisms and organizations develop, they become more and more structured, with more and more interconnections and control mechanisms governing the flows of matter, energy, and information.
- Highly structured or complex systems may have long delays in the flow of information so that consequences may occur some time after the originating action.

> When a highly-structured system experiences a significant change (which may be large or small, depending on its cycles) in flows of energy, matter, and information, the system may break down into smaller units or may "suddenly" restructure into a hierarchically more advanced form, in which complexity is less apparent and information flows are increased while matter and energy flows and structures are decreased.

Taken together, these ideas comprise the essence of what is called "whole systems thinking." They offer a model of our lives and of our planet with a very different set of processes and expectations than most of us grew up with or were taught in school. But when we think about them, they make sense—far more sense than much of what we've been taught. And, as we begin to think in this way, our actions in the world are different.

Expanding the Understanding

Fortunately, bits and pieces of these ideas are being taught in Western schools, as ecology, as organizational behavior, as computer science, and to some extent as physiology and biophysics. Unfortunately, these are bits and pieces, scattered widely across a curriculum that is still divided into subject areas that appear to contradict the basic concept:

> the universe is one whole system of which we are part and in which we must always experience consequences for our observation, action, and inaction.

Sadly, the result of their piecemeal education is that our political, social, and economic leaders continue to address things in a piecemeal fashion without taking long-term consequences into account—in spite of environmental regulations requiring the analysis of long-term effects—and humanity's presence on the planet appears to become less sustainable every day.

Still, since the 1980s, as these ideas have been tried, tested, modeled on computers, explored in longevity studies, they've been proven to be the most accurate model of how organisms, organizations, and the universe operate.

Then, in the 1990s a new idea began to emerge: the idea that the underlying universal system is, in fact, the quantum field out of which both matter and energy emerge, and throughout which there appears to be a form of intelligence at work. The now-observable underlying order in what once were considered chaotic processes contributed in large part to this merger of quantum theory and systems thinking, as did the observations of dissipative structures in both organic and inorganic systems.[40]

I was very fortunate to be involved in this field of study during these decades, and to work with a number of its leading-edge thinkers and contributors. As a student, as a professor and designer of curriculum (I helped create the program at Antioch-Seattle where Milt received his Master's degree, among others), and as a consultant working with government agencies and non-profit organizations, I've had the opportunity to explore, apply, and clarify my own and others' understanding of systems. Along the way, we've created new models of thinking and new approaches to problems that have taken us beyond anything we thought possible before. As a result this is, for me, a living body of ideas—not just something I read in a book that is now considered "sacred." Because I've met many of the people and heard their stories—even participated in some of their concept development—it's alive in my world. In a way, we might say that for me, Systems Thinking is a "living language," in the same way that the Hebrew language was for the Israelites before it was written down and codified.

Today, I'm fascinated to watch as the systems field is on the edge of proving what Indigenous peoples have always known: we are a part of something much greater than we can conceive, with an intelligence far beyond our own, and if we observe carefully we can learn to harmonize our thinking and actions with that intelligence and begin to see that intelligence at work in our world. Then, I'm hoping, we can learn to apply its processes in our lives in ways that are mutually beneficial for the immediate and long-term wellbeing of all humanity.

---

[40] Fritjof Capra's book, *The Web of Life*, and *Mind Walk*, a film he and his brother produced, are very effective introductions to these ideas. Also Amit Goswami's *Quantum Activist*, both the book and the dvd.

Living Systems: The Theory Underlying Sustainability

"The present disintegration of the life systems of the Earth is so extensive that we might very well be bringing an end to the Cenozoic period that has provided the identity for the life process of Earth during the past sixty-seven million years. During that period life expanded with amazing fluorescence prior to the coming of the human." ~ *Thomas Berry & Brian Swimme* [41]

Milt Markewitz

Prologue

It's my belief that being in touch with life and its processes is absolutely essential if we're ever to attain a sustainable existence.

For many this is primarily a spiritual quest, but I think it is also an intellectual and academic one, if we're to understand what makes a living system a living system; what brings and takes life from the systems in which we are immersed; how language informs our perceptions; and how we expand our insights so that this newly acquired knowledge resonates in terms of individual and collective ethics and guiding principles. This section will articulate my own personal motivation, a Living Systems curriculum I've developed, subsequent work I've done that has me convinced that there is very important learning to be done, and how my individual beliefs have emerged as a result of learning about the collective Indigenous peoples' internalizing of balance, harmony and sacred ecology.

Following my retirement from IBM in 1991, I became very interested in the mystical traditions, including my own Judaic tradition of Qabala. In concert with this work I became convinced that we are an ecologically unsustainable culture, and that then

---

[41] Thomas Berry & Brian Swimme, *The Universe Story* p. 3

led me to seek to understand how we are also socially and economically unsustainable.

In the late 1990s a friend called me and asked if I'd have dinner with him. He wanted to share an idea that he'd lived with for years and had only shared with a couple of other people. After ordering dinner, he gave me a copy of an article written by Willis Harman, then President of the Institute for Noetic Sciences, regarding the consciousness of all living systems, and asked me if it was of interest to me. I was surprised by my own response: an enthusiasm that came from deep inside me.

My friend Jerry Kasinger's idea was to build greenhouse structures using state of the art technology for creating a nurturing environment and developing a relationship with nature that facilitated growing quantities of nourishing food that could be harvested daily to feed a whole family.

I worked diligently with Jerry as we focused on creating our business plan, raising capital, a manufacturing plan that included developing a prototype, and a marketing plan.

The learning was intense as we were truly a leading edge application in a transformational paradigm shift. We were inventing a technology that advocated a change from corporate farming, with all its inherent centralized control and distribution logistics, to personal/family production, consumption, and control. As intriguing and difficult as it was to manufacture our first-phase product, which we called a 'Garden Pod,' and to design all the technology for the second phase—making the 'Pod' as reliant as possible on its own energy, water and nurturing systems—my heart was in Phase Three, essentially emulating nature's consciousness.

After almost two years of working together, we received the venture capital we needed to get started, honed our manufacturing processes and built a prototype, completed design of the technology necessary to embark on the second phase, and brought on board a staff of bright, dedicated young folk. I had done what I could with my limited knowledge, and the seeds had literally been planted that could only be nurtured with a deeper understanding of the consciousness of all life.

That's when I entered the Whole System Design master's degree program, then at Antioch University in Seattle—starting on 9/11/2001.

My cohort of students at Antioch was introduced to Living Systems Theory shortly after we started, and this became the framework for almost all my subsequent learning. Each year the cohort was split up into several Design Teams that were responsible for researching a subject and, along with guest faculty, teaching that subject to our cohort. In the spring of 2003 my Design Team subject was Living Systems, and we had the privilege of co-teaching with Dr. Fritjof Capra.

The challenge we faced was to take one particular understanding of Living Systems, developed by two Chilean biologists, Drs. Humberto Maturana and Francisco Varela, and simplify it greatly without losing its essence. I had thought about this quite a bit when I had the privilege of discussing this work with a guest professor, Dr. Pille Bunnell, a colleague and co-author with Drs. Maturana and Varela. We met for lunch one day to talk about how we might develop Living System curricula for elementary and high school students. Pille remains a mentor and has contributed immensely to my learning as I've progressed with this work.

The Design Team observed living systems at a macro-level, rather than the cellular level described by Maturana and Varela, and identified 5 attributes that we found were relatively easy to understand through a combination of explanation, getting in touch with personal life experiences, and embodiment. I've subsequently added my understanding of the flow of all living systems by simplifying the 'Panarchy' work of C. S. "Buzz" Holling and his colleagues, and included my learning regarding the life processes that emerge from my understanding of the ancient Hebrew language.

This combination of concepts became the basis for my own Living Systems curriculum. In my brief foray into teaching 5th through 12th grade students, I found that they could understand the basics of Living Systems in a single class period using this approach, and I think some form of this work should be included at all levels of our education system. Here's what I showed them.

A Living Systems Curriculum

Autopoietic Attributes

The word used to describe all living systems is 'autopoietic.' An autopoietic system is:

- A recursive organization that creates continuously its own organization
- Manifesting a continually changing structure
- Maintaining its own boundary
- Continually renewing, cleansing, and healing

And these characteristics may be seen in the ongoing processes of all Living Systems.

Composting and Re-composing

In Nature, our ecological base, there is zero waste. Every living system is biodegradable and when it dies, it recomposes as sustenance for other living systems. So dissipation doesn't lead to the demise of a system, but is an integral part of an ongoing process in which new forms are constantly re-emerging. And what emerges is part of an ongoing adaptation and improvement process. Thus, contrary to our thermodynamic understanding of entropy—everything must break down into dust—life flourishes.

Emergence

Living systems that are suited to their environment flourish. They interact in such a way that there is novelty. Chemically, hydrogen and oxygen, neither with apparent properties of water, combine to form water; animals like bees become part of the flora's proliferation process, as well as create honey; natural forces like the wind interact with the trees to help them develop tensile strength. We are surrounded by a plethora of newness every day. Unlike mechanical systems where the whole is always less than the sum of its parts, it appears that in living systems, the whole is always greater than the sum of its parts. There are elements of surprise, novelty and mystery.

Structural Coupling

There is a web of life and we are more than just connected. We are highly interdependent. Our species relies on the trees for oxygen just as the trees rely on us for carbon dioxide. We rely on the Earth's systems to sustain our lives—clouds to filter us from the sun; cleansing for suitable water, air and soil; growing for food and materials; and healing that for our species comes from sensual beauty and naturopathic medicines; and for the Earth's systems from an innate intelligence grounded in a blending of competition and cooperation where cooperation is the dominant paradigm. We are energetically connected with every other living system.

Reproduction

Each living system has the capacity to reproduce itself so that the integrity of its structure is maintained. A pattern exists between parents and offspring and across species for all time. Yet each offspring is unique.

Organization and Structure

In mechanical systems, structure is fixed and we believe we control change by controlling structures and re-organizations. In living systems, the organization seems to be based on a fixed set of processes while the structure is in constant flux.

Considering these characteristics and processes in light of Suares' matrix, the similarities become quite clear, and several questions arise:

➢ Are these life processes integrally imbedded in ancient and indigenous languages?

➢ Are they specifically found in the ancient Hebrew as expressed by the 9 columns of Suares' matrix in "The Cipher of Genesis"?

➢ Are these the necessary and sufficient conditions to create and sustain all life?

➢ And is our challenge to flow with, rather than try to manage, the emergent changes?

It is interesting to note how the 9 columns from Suares' matrix not only define the life processes with which all life is endowed, but easily map into the 5 attributes of Living Systems described in our curriculum.

Autopoesis	Life Processes
Re-Composing: Life	Life-death cycle
Emergence	Energy & Possibilities
Structural Coupling	Universal Life & Attraction
Reproduction	Fertilization, Incubation & Birthing
Organization & Structure	Perfect Order

Living Systems Flow

The following graphic is a simplified version synthesized from the book, *Panarchy: Understanding Transformations in Human and Natural Systems*, written by C. S. "Buzz" Holling and several colleagues. They each studied a large natural system such as reefs, savannahs, and glaciers, and would meet periodically to compare notes. The graphic shows that all Living Systems have a natural flow that not only helps us understand systems, but also provides great insight for interventions in their processes.

THE GENERIC FLOW OF PANARCHY

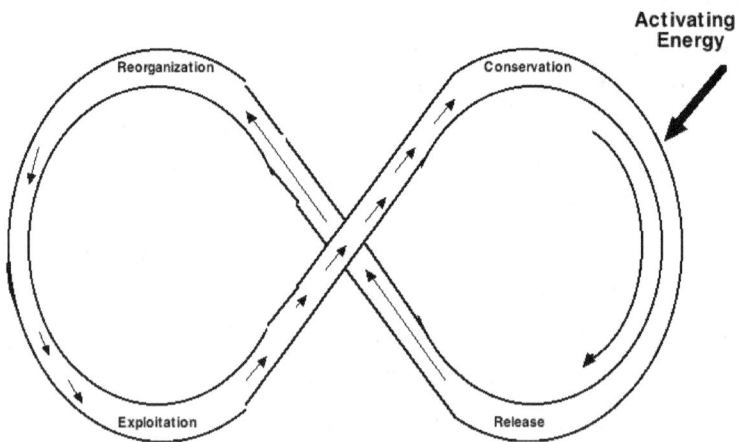

In order to analyze the never-ending Panarchy cycle, begin with the "Activating Energy" that perturbs the system with energy that "awakens" and nurtures latent seeds. Following this is an immediate "Release" quickly followed by "Reorganization" activities, and then the slower processes of the system being fertile and sustaining other new life ("Exploitation"), before moving into a more dormant stage ("Conservation"). These cycles are geological, like eruptions and earthquakes, epochal like forests, annual like our seasons, or as short as nanoseconds in the case of particles. The cycles are nested, so there may be an extremely large number of smaller cycles within a larger cycle.

How does Nature Organize?

My assumptions about Nature's organization stem to a large degree from Dee Hock's work on the 'chaord', a term he coined to describe systems that may be perceived as chaotic at one level, but are actually ordered when discerned from a different perspective. Hock described 'chaordic' as, "the behavior of a self-governing organism or system that harmoniously blends what were previously conceived to be opposites, such as chaos and order, or cooperation and competition."[42] He writes that chaordic systems have the following attributes:

- An elegantly simple structure
- Clear purpose
- Grounded in guiding principles
- Blend apparent opposites

Teaching the Curriculum

When I teach Living Systems to K-12 students, I find that these ideas are readily understood—as if there's an awakening of an already existing inner knowledge—and they provide a basis for learning about specific topics like permaculture, hydroponics, and natural resource management as well as provides a basis for observing all life phenomena. The students experience a paradigm shift as they discern their world as organic rather than mechanical

---

[42] 'What is Enlightenment' Interview, http://www.wie.org/j22hockintro.asp

and recognize that all systems are living systems with embedded mechanical processes. They more clearly see their connection to place and community, and I think glimpse the importance of language to furthering their understanding. From all this students become more in touch with their sense of purpose.

From an educational perspective, then, I've come to believe that recognizing that Living Systems is the theory that underlies sustainability is critical, and that internalizing what it means to be alive provides the incentive to live the ethics required for sustainability.

Where Western education tends to be highly segmented into subjects, class periods, teacher specialization, and separation from community and family, the new approach begins with the organic structures of environment, family and community as the classroom, and integrate fixed structures such as classrooms, teacher specialization, laboratories and testing where they are deemed to be the best approach to learning. While standards are largely set by the requirements of the schools and organizations to which our students aspire, those we set for ourselves will be to support the improvement process that is paramount for learning.

The objective is to create life long learners, and cultures that are in every way sustainable. Suggested learning topics include Appreciative Inquiry (more on that soon), Bio-Mimicry, and Holling's Panarchy cycle, described above. Perhaps the most important learning is Living Systems, for this is the theory that underlies sustainability and when we understand it, we also understand the ethics required to be sustainable.

After teaching one class of high school juniors and seniors, I received the following feedback, which I think indicates the importance of offering these ideas to teens and preteens.

> Hi Milt,
>
> Thanks again for generously sharing with us… In response to the question, "What is something from Theory of Knowledge that gave you hope?" a student named Natural Systems thinking as the most powerful. He described how after reading Ishmael, he felt discouraged like we are all damned if we do and damned if we don't. Systems thinking provided

him a strategy to respond to the challenges of our world. Another student, when asked which class she'd like to live over, said she would choose your presentation to integrate it more fully. We had a great discussion prompted by your talk, and I told them that if we had to boil the entire course down to one day, I would choose your presentation as most representative of the most important ideas. I look forward to having you in earlier next year -- maybe October or November?--and if it works in your schedule, for 90 minutes instead of 50…

Best,

Kent ((Siebold), Cleveland HS, 'Theory of Knowledge' teacher)

Applying the Theory

In the previous chapter, I stated that one of our three needed paradigm shifts was to change our primary science from Newtonian physics to Living Systems, but the shift is much broader than that. With the recognition that all systems are living systems, we can begin to look at all our organizations, institutions, groups, and conversations as alive. We can be more effective by designing for emergence—after all isn't this what learning is all about? And we can discern much more clearly how to intervene with organizational problems when we ask what brings, and takes, life from the system, and map our organizational behaviors onto the Panarchic cycle. As Kurt Lewin so profoundly stated, "There is nothing so practical as a good theory."[43]

Based on the ideas expressed in the 'Organization and Structure' paragraph above, I've inferred that inherent in Nature's organization is a set of life processes with which all living systems have been blessed, and that an understanding of these gifts is inherent in some, perhaps all, ancient languages.

As is evident in my "Binding of Isaac" story, told earlier in this book, I think it's very important to reflect on the possibility of cultures that through their language have an understanding of life, and know at the deepest level the sacredness of ecology.

---

[43] http://psychology.about.com/od/psychologyquotes/a/lewinquotes.htm

These are the wisdom cultures described in the previous chapter of this book. They understand their personal and collective responsibility to maintain balance and harmony, and recognize it as the basis for ecological sustainability, as well as social wellness and economic viability.

The Living Systems Experience

My understanding of Living Systems has no doubt made it easier for me to work with and learn from Native American colleagues, and I'd like to share a couple experiences that informed me just how differently we think and act.

No Longer Mechanical

A few years ago I had the opportunity to present Living Systems to Mr. Joe Finkbonner, Executive Director of the Northwest Portland Area Health Board, and as I was leaving he put his hand on my shoulder and said, "I'm going to file this under mechanical." We laughed, and I thought how perfect that Joe understands organically what I feel needs to be academically expressed to the perponderance of students in our Western education systems.

Living Land or Preserved Landscape?

The second experience happened a couple months before finalizing this book, while visiting a segment of land purchased by our Portland Metro-area governance office. It was a combination of farmland, forest, and wetlands located about 10 miles south of Portland.

The land had been left to its natural ways for a relatively short time and a perfusion of native plants had emerged. It appeared that latent seeds that had been dormant for decades now flourished when left alone to do so. I'd describe the Metro folks who were our hosts as extremely earthy, treehuggers, whose life-work was all about restoration and ecological sustainability.

As I walked the land I made a point of walking with Mr. David Lewis, one of several attending members of the Confererated Tribes of Grand Ronde, to try and understand what he was thinking and observing. He shared with me a deep appreciation for Metro and the people who had worked so hard to protect this land and let it flourish naturally. And he also expressed that the land without people with an ancestral understanding of the plants and terrain was incomplete. He shared with me how certain plants would be harvested and treated so that they would become a part of village life—medicines, materials for weaving, and all the other functions necessary for humans to flourish while accepting their responsibility for maintaining balance and harmony.

David helped me understand how integral human activities are to bringing life to this place, and how there was a sense that perhaps the Western sense of preservation had an ornamental feel—like a zoo or plant collection, rather than a living, growing, being.

Hope

"The conscious emulation of life's genius is a survival strategy for the human race, a path to a sustainable future. The more our world functions like the natural world, the more likely we are to endure on this home that is ours, but not ours alone." ~ *Janine Benyus*[44]

Milt Markewitz

Often, when I speak to groups about sustainability, some of the attendees become quite sad and express their sense of hopelessness, depression and inability to move forth. Their rationale usually emanates from powerful cultural Western norms of hierarchy, economic driving forces that lead to ecological dominion, and social injustice, as well as the inability by many leaders to accept responsibility for how our societal ways have devastated the planet.

I find that the following graphics and ideas generally instill a spark of hope, and sometimes expressions of very deep gratitude.

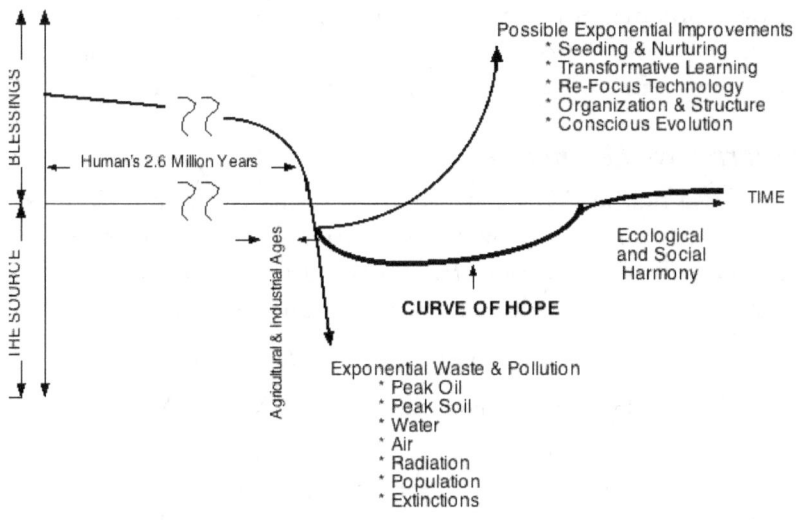

---

[44] Janine Benyus on the website: www.biomimicryinstitute.org

If we only consider the curve on the left, 'Exponential Waste and Pollution,' it's easy to understand why folks are depressed, and, it should be noted, each bullet listed is a very serious problem that we are faced with today. In fact the last bullet, extinctions, are occurring at the highest rate since meteors wiped out the dinosaurs. We have to wonder if our own species can survive the relatively recent devastation of what has been, for the millennia of the existence of life, a very nurturing planet.

Moving along the Curve of Hope

My initial approach to offsetting our current exponential waste and pollution cycle was to draw the 'Curve of Hope' graph and then define improvements we might initiate. A colleague, Mark Maggiora, helped me understand that 'Exponential Waste & Pollution' must be systemically offset with 'Exponential Improvements,' together creating an emergent 'Curve of Hope.'

The Possible Exponential Improvements that are listed on the up-curve in the graph can be understood as follows.

Seeding and Nurturing

Inherent here is the shift from a mechanical assumption to an organic processes orientation, and we begin to discern our institutions, organizations, projects and conversations as alive and our primary work is to assure vitality. The study of Living Systems is most critical if we are to infuse vitality into all we do.

Transformative Learning

Because neither Western nor Indigenous cultures widely use the term 'Learning Organizations,' perhaps this is the place to begin. We can redefine our structures, curricula, and instruction to welcome surprises by helping students understand:

- o How to develop their own 'Personal Mastery'
- o How to understand and use 'Mental Models'
- o How to work together through 'Team Learning'—people learn different possibilities when they different ways of seeing things, doing things, presenting things

o How to develop "Shared Visions" that blend the timeless virtues of the Indigenous cultures with the goals and objectives of the Western approach

o How to use 'Systems Thinking' that expects relationships and flows to be as important as objects, includes the several Human Dynamics perspectives, suspends disbelief, operates in creative tension, and utilizes dialogue as an emergent learning tool.[45]

Re-Focus Technology

Western education has a great deal to offer in terms of understanding current technology and how it is applied. The question for the Indigenous Peoples is how to apply the technology without disrupting the essence of their culture. Where technology, like dams, has been applied that has seriously disrupted cultures, what are the design points for the replacement technology? Also, the application of ever improving Internet capabilities will be essential to assure both access to all learners, and the capacity to create, adapt and share best curricula and instruction practices. Organizationally, the Western world was impelled to re-focus its technologies from production, such as cars, to warring vehicles during WWII, and now it is time to shift again to apply technology to solving sustainability problems.

Reconfigure Organization & Structure

This most crucial area requires that we understand how Nature is organized, that competition and cooperation are blended and that cooperation is the primary paradigm. Perhaps this is best understood in terms of the games of life that we all play. As we saw above, the myriad of 'finite' games governed by rules and always with winners and losers, and the 'infinite' games that are governed by guiding principles like being in harmony with the Earth and each other.

---

[45] The above terminology is taken from Peter M. Senge's, *The Fifth Discipline: The Art and Practice of the Learning Organization.*

All this is well understood by the indigenous peoples, and it's crucial for democracies because they only work when individuals let go of short-term "win/lose" strategies in favor of long-term guiding principles. In the U.S., our Constitution contains our guiding principles.

Also, natural organic systems are different from mechanical systems in a single very profound way. In mechanical systems structures are fixed and the processes to which they're applied are constantly eroding and wearing down, whereas in organic systems there seem to be a set of processes with which all forms of life are endowed, and the organic structures are in constant flux and development.

Conscious Evolution

This is our ultimate goal: to make the paradigm shifts necessary to once more be in harmony with ourselves, our planet, and the people around us, to re-create the relatively pristine ecological environments that existed before the Industrial Age, and to facilitate the emergence of just and peaceful societies.

Here we can look again at the 'Archetypes for Sustainability' and see how the infusion of Indigenous wisdom into each of the three 'Knowledge Quadrants'–'Business,' 'Colonizer' and 'Social Action'—is necessary if each quadrant and the whole system are to be sustainable. I learned to discern this when a First Nations' person explained to me that the quadrant in the upper left-hand corner, 'Colonizing' or 'Power,' looked completely different when viewed through the indigenous lens and that power could emanate in a communal, cooperative fashion and be a paradigm of peace.

The primary shift in the 'Business' quadrant is significantly reducing with accumulation and individual wealth, and to be able to discern expenses holistically, without externalities.

Finally, the 'Social Action' learns from Nature to blend apparent opposites, and to develop ethics of mutuality and what brings life and its inherent happiness.

Putting the Curve to Work

When I was asked to design a Colloquium called 'Limits to Growth,' the 'Curve of Hope' graphic served as the primary design document. We selected three speakers, each of whom had a world-view that we thought matched a single portion of the curve. Our first speaker articulated a position of being so far down the 'Exponential Waste & Pollution Curve' that we have no hope of ever surviving what we have wrought. The second speaker chose to articulate potential success in terms of developing a shared vision followed by a plan with goals, objectives and measurements rather than 'Exponential Improvements.' And the third speaker, Mr. Larry Merculieff, of the Aleut Nation of Pribilof Island of St. Paul in the Bering Sea, eloquently enlightened all of us. His perspective of being in ecological and social harmony is based on principles, ethics and virtues that are timeless. The virtues of the past that have been lived for centuries are the same virtues we want for our children and all the generations that follow, and in order to achieve these virtues, he reiterated several times, we must live them every day.

Starting with principles, ethics, and virtues is very different from the normal Western approach of an individual identifying a vision and engaging others to achieve it, or even the more modern approach of defining a shared vision developed primarily around goals and objectives, and creating a plan with measurements and milestones. It's not starting with the problem and defining solutions.

The 'Curve of Hope' can be used from either perspective, and these very different approaches may need to be blended. My suggestion is that the shared vision be developed based primarily on principles, ethics and virtues, rather than goals and objectives, and that we make a conscious effort to replace external measurements with personal and communal ethics and intrinsic motivation.

Appreciative Inquiry-Ecological Harmony

"What would happen to our change practices if we began all of our work with positive presumption – that organizations, as centers of human relatedness, are "alive" with infinite constructive capacity?" ~ *David Cooperrider*[46]

Milt Markewitz

Living within Nature's limits to renew, cleanse, and heal is absolutely essential for the well-being of humanity. Only then are we living sustainably.

This understanding of sustainability leads us to question the widely accepted definition of sustainability that was developed by the Brundtland Commission of the United Nations on March 20, 1987:

> Sustainable development is development that meets the needs of the present without compromising the ability of future generations to meet their own needs.

This definition is attributed to an Iroquois spokesman to the Commission, but, based on what we've been saying here, in all likelihood misses the essence of his message. His context was one of 7 generations, and he included two bullet points that he said were essential. One referred to the need for ecological limitations and the other to social equity.

The question is: "Can all 7 billion human inhabitants of the planet live in balance and harmony, or are there just too many of us to do so—or are there too many of us who refuse to change unsustainable life styles?"

Answering this question requires that we be clear about what sustainable means. And, in accordance what the concepts shared in the last chapter, I suggest that any definition of sustainability

---

[46] David Cooperrider et al, *Appreciative Inquiry: An Emerging Direction of Organizational Development*, p.6

not be written to 'meet needs,' but to incorporate the following guiding principles:

> ➤ Ecological Harmony—living within Nature's limits to renew, cleanse and heal, and

> ➤ Social Harmony—communities, local to global, who are governed by ethics of peace, sufficiency, sharing, and supporting the common good.

By including both of these we can take what previously looked to be impossible and re-frame it. We may even be able to reframe our approach to re-achieving sustainability of the planet.

Doing the Impossible

My colleague, Jeff Goebel, has been very successful over the years with 'doing the impossible,' and I was fortunate to be in a 'Community Consensus Workshop' addressing our salmon-sea lion dilemma at the ladders that the salmon use to get past a dam where I experienced his approach. He told us that in order to frame either a best case or worse case scenario, the parameters must already be present for us. The dilemma being addressed here has a worst case of our planet Earth being decimated so that it no longer supports human existence; and the best case is expressed in the 'Curve of Hope' where we live in balance and harmony and every decision we make is guided by the appropriate ethics. When framed this way, the task doesn't look impossible at all. Peoples lived this way for tens of thousands of years, and the wisdom necessary to be that way again is available. Discerning the possibility of success enhances our will to make the necessary changes.

Over the years I've found that one of the most powerful attributes of good leadership is reframing situations so that what may have been overwhelming may in fact be relatively easy, enlightening and freeing for those who experience it. I would like to share an experience of my own that succeeded in every way by those who reframed their understanding of a situation, share a little about the process that was applied, and a most important facet of that process that is often overlooked in our Western culture.

The Fairview A-I Process

The project that met the requirement for my graduation from the Whole System Design program at Antioch University stemmed from a conversation I'd had with our State School Superintendent regarding an Executive Order by our Governor to achieve a sustainable State by 2025. My question to her was: "How do our sustainability efforts in Oregon inform public education, and what role will our public schools play in achieving our State goal?"

Based on that conversation, I set out to find a small community and its school system to work together to define both a sustainable future and the learning that would need to take place both in the school and the community. Through a colleague, Dr. Ed Smith, in the Reynolds School District just east of Portland, I found a school with the ideal principal, Patricia Martinez. My initial work was to cement relationships with Patricia and the city planners in Fairview, Oregon where her school is located.

In May of 2002 our visiting professor at Antioch Seattle was Dr. David Cooperrider, the developer of Appreciative Inquiry (A-I). We were given readings on the subject prior to class and I took the time to reflect on how I might incorporate the process into my Antioch graduation project. David shared with us a story of doing his own PhD studies and going to a medical clinic in Cleveland where he asked employees a very neutral question regarding their work. 90% or more answered in terms of a problem with which they were dealing, while less than 10% told of how they were doing their life work and the fulfillment they received. David's thesis was the beginning of A-I, an authentic process for surfacing virtues while acknowledging problems, and coming to action in ways that do what needs doing yet in a manner consistent with one's principles.

I was so taken with A-I that, in parallel with my Antioch studies, I enrolled in a year-long A-I Certification program facilitated by Dr. Cooperrider and his mentor, Dr. Ron Frye. Since becoming certified, I have used A-I extensively for opening meetings, conversation groups, classes and workshops, for fundraising at my synagogue, and as the basis for design of the 'Caring for

Creation' track at a United Religions Initiative North American Conference. Gratitude for all life is at the heart of this book, and Appreciative Inquiry is an incredible tool for developing this appreciative way of being.

Appreciative Inquiry was used extensively and successfully to enroll faculty, parents, and a Steering Committee at Fairview. Our project, 'Imagine Fairview' was to a degree modeled after a similar project, "Imagine Chicago.' Our plan had three phases:

1. Convene a Community Meeting to hear of the city's vision and articulate it from a sustainable perspective.
2. Work with the educators to develop curricula and instruction for both the school and the city.
3. Set up an ongoing education and implementation program.

For now, suffice it to say that Phase 1 of the project was a very big success. A-I was used as the starting point in meetings, interviews, and in the Community Meeting we held. Some examples of its application follow.

Appreciative Inquiry in Action

In order to get the faculty to buy into the project, I asked Patricia if I could have half an hour of her next staff meeting to get their commitment. She obliged, and when I met with the faculty, I asked them for their cooperation in discovering what brings life to their jobs.

I developed a very simple Appreciative Inquiry that asked each teacher to get in touch with a deeply moving moment in their own learning, one that was an incredible 'aha,' and that both influenced them to be teachers and continues to influence how they teach today. They paired up and each was allotted three minutes to share their experiences. The energy was palpable, and once quieted, we talked about the experience of sharing their stories.

Two points were made that I'll probably never forget. First, a young man said, "I didn't understand what you meant when you said, 'What brings life to my job,' and now I know." And then a group of teachers converged on the notion that they wanted appreciation to be a virtue in their culture.

I think a little of the joy of this 'discovery' is recognizing that everyone in the room had such a story, they were delighted to tell it, and even more delighted that there was deep listening. The storytelling experience created a strong bond within each pair, and the later sharing connected everyone.

Through this process I confirmed a strong intuitive feeling that it makes far more sense to experience A-I then to try to learn about it through reading or a presentation. The same experiential approach was used when I met with PTA members, the planning team we pulled together, and many of the city folks from Fairview.

Community Invitation

Almost every Fairview citizen with whom I met told me that my Community Meeting would never work. They told me of the social rifts within their community: old timers vs. recent arrivals, geographical disputes, and social status differences. I told each of them that I trusted the process, and that I believed the A-I bonding would mitigate their simmering differences. I'm very happy to say that I was correct, because I have doubts about my own facilitation skills when there is conflict. Where other facilitators might focus on conflict resolution, I've found that A-I is a terrific tool for minimizing and often avoiding conflict.

One of the most incredible uses of A-I was for inviting people to our Community Meeting. Our tact was to have students do inter-generational interviews, and we developed age appropriate Appreciative Inquiries with the following theme:

> Please think of someone who you very much appreciate and perhaps you haven't either thanked them or told them the depth of your gratitude. Please call this person, thank them and request an interview. The primary question is: "What inspired you to perform the act of kindness?" Listen attentively to what they have to say and take only enough notes so that you'll remember the gist of their story; thank them for their time and for their kindness and invite them to our Community Meeting.

The smaller children usually picked a parent or a teacher, and the feedback was always positive and very sweet.

I worked with a high school economics class whose students came back with the most incredible stories, many of which brought tears to our eyes. One big, tough young man's experience was of someone who had brought him a glass of water on a very hot day when he was doing yard work. When he asked his benefactor what inspired this act of kindness, the man told him that when he was young he used to always fight with his brothers. One day, quite suddenly, their father passed away, and the brothers realized how important they were to each other. He said that the brothers never fought again, and he had become a kinder person. It struck me that this and other stories, in addition to being very powerful, had an organic feel. They often didn't have the linear cause and effect that I'd grown to expect in stories.

When we finished hearing each student, the teacher, Ms. Jennifer Faro, was obviously deeply touched, and she shared two points with the class. First, she asked if anyone could relate what we'd just done with the economic theories and equations they'd been learning. None of them could. She explained that the theories and equations they were learning would be necessary to know when they entered the workforce, and of course they needed to know them to pass her tests. But, more importantly, if they were to advance in their work and solve more complex problems, it was the appreciation of people and relationship building that was at the heart of a strong, effective organization. Her second comment was that this class would never be the same again, that what they had shared and the appreciation they had for each other would positively affect their learning together.

We had completed the 'Definition' phase of A-I with our invitation process and in the process set the theme and the tone for our 1-day Community Meeting.

When the Community Meeting actually happened, almost 80 townspeople participated and were genuinely excited to both share their stories and focus on the future of their community. I was feeling more and more like I could overcome the 'impossible.'

Meeting Process

The agenda for the Community Meeting followed the A-I Cycle as it flows from phase to phase.

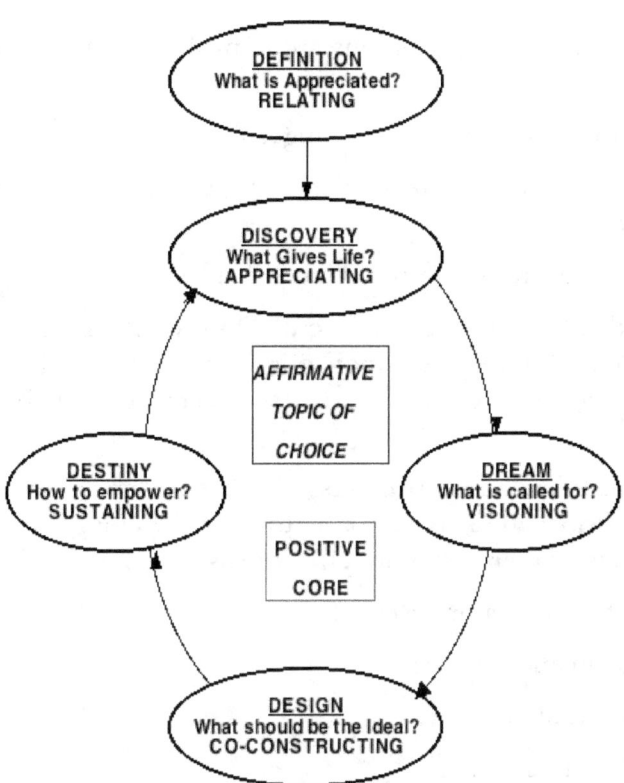

This graphic is the Appreciative Inquiry schematic that I used to design the Meeting. The 'Definition' phase is one I added to the normal 4-phase cycle for our invitation process described above. The 'Discovery', 'Dream', 'Design', and 'Destiny' phases of the A-I process always revolve around a well-defined 'Affirmative Topic of Choice' and a set of agreed-on guiding principles and agreed upon virtues named the 'Positive Core'.

After a welcome from the principal, Patricia Martinez, we began our communal work with the step called 'Discovery'. The use of A-I intended to put people in touch with their caring for the Fairview Community and their sense of place. When that was completed, I told them about the A-I Process and how it would be central for the rest of our work that day. We discussed the 'Affirmative Topic of Choice' and 'Creating Fairview as a Sustainable Community', and we reviewed four Key Principles that were our 'Positive Core:'

1) People and organizations aren't problems but sources of Wisdom;

2) Avoidance of all Deficit Language;

3) Inclusion of all stakeholders in a Relational Environment; and

4) Reconnection with our 'Latent' Virtues.

We added the virtues from our 'Discovery' process to the Key Principles, and agreed upon our 'Positive Core'. I then reviewed our agenda for the day that consisted of the following segments:

The Fairview town planners presented a document called 'Fairview Vision 2022' as the basis for our dreaming. We developed 6 facets of their vision in terms of sustainability attributes:

1) Protecting Natural Resources,

2) Sustainable Industries,

3) Renewable Energy,

4) Public Recreation,

5) Revitalizing Downtown, and

6) Strengthening Community

Since we only had a limited amount of time, participants selected two facilitated conversation topics; one from the first three sustainability attributes, and one from the last three. Following these conversations everyone met to share what the participants had developed, from which we had the framework for the 'Design" phase.

We closed with an appreciative reflection and sharing process intended to give everyone a new sense of what our 'Destiny' might now be.[1]

Transformation & Transcendence

As I continue to use A-I as a relationship building tool whenever I design or facilitate a gathering, I find that people are transformed when they connect with their most cherished virtues, and they love to tell their stories. Often individuals after experiencing sharing an intimate story with someone they've never met before will say something to the effect, "I feel as if I've just met a soul-mate." And often a whole community will be transformed by the experience of sharing, and then following that with 'Dreaming', Designing' and then feeling a new sense of 'Destiny', defined as "the inner purpose of a life that can be discovered and realized."

Clearly we are capable of grounding our lives in Sacred Ecology—the appreciation, gratitude, and acceptance of our responsibility to be in concert with the Earth as it cleanses and heals to provide pristine water, air, and soil so life forms of all kinds might flourish.

In Dr. Richard Tarnas' article, "Romancing the Cosmos," in the 12/2005–2/2006 IONS *Shift* Magazine, he suggests the possibility to reframe our destiny. He writes that our universe is 'a deeply-souled, subtly mysterious cosmos of great spiritual beauty and creative intelligence.' He goes on to create an understanding that when we view the cosmos 'as being at least as intelligent and noble, as worthy a being, as permeated with mind and soul, as imbued with moral aspiration and purpose, as endowed with spiritual depths and mystery' as we are, then we might find the mutuality to unite 'and thereby bring forth something new, a creative synthesis'. Dr. Tarnas suggests that what emerges may be

> a new capacity for self-transcendence, both intellectual and moral, so that we may experience a new dimension of beauty and intelligence in the world – not a projection of our own desire for beauty and intellectual mastery, but an encounter with

the actual unpredictability, unfolding beauty, and intelligence of the whole.[47]

Overcoming the impossible is often just a state of mind. Having a tool like Appreciative Inquiry helped me see this.

---

[1] Unfortunately, the project was terminated shortly after the Community Meeting for the following reasons. First, the city determined that they didn't have the money or staff to continue their support. I had made a tactical error by finding a school first, and then going to the city planners where the school was located. I believe that each city or town must self-select so that they are motivated, and there should be a qualification process to be sure that they are committed and ready to move forth. Second, the teachers said that they had to remain too focused on achieving Oregon's standards oriented programs to develop new curricula on their own. I asked my school district colleague, Ed Smith to join me in making a case with the Oregon Department of Education for the fundamental structural changes necessary to support schools who wished to participate in projects like 'Imagine Fairview'. We met with a mutual colleague, Dr. Pat Burke, the Assistant State School Superintendent, described our project and the varied ways we'd integrated Appreciative Inquiry. He was very interested and asked us to send him additional materials. We asked him to support a process where schools could develop curriculum, like that necessary to achieve balanced sustainability, and collaborate among schools. New standards would emerge from their work, and folded into the current process as applicable.

Dr. Burke said that he couldn't help us because of the other problems with which he was dealing – particularly in light of all the other financial and legislative issues.

I believe that we were just a little ahead of our time, and as municipalities become more focused on sustainability and schools come to terms with how our sustainability efforts inform public education and visa versa, we can dust off the project, revise it, and have a model for seeding and nurturing sustainability at the heart of each community—the schools.

---

[47] Richard Tarnas, "Romancing the Cosmos," *Shift* Magazine, Institute of Noetic Sciences, 12/2005–2/2006, p. 35-37.

Grace & Gratitude

Ruth Miller

Prologue

When Milt introduced me to Appreciative Inquiry I was struck by the essential similarity it had to a blessing ceremony or invocation. As he shared it with me, I heard "start with asking people what they appreciate about what you're focusing on, then explore what they'd like to experience more of, then how they'd like to experience that, and finally what they appreciated about the process." And, as he shared some of the successes he'd had using the process, I thought of all the rituals and ceremonies I'd been part of (or led) that began and ended with "Thank you" to all the material and spiritual beings present for all that transpired. And I remembered that once, when I was assessing the economic history of the U.S., I had observed that our economy began to suffer at just about the same point in history that Americans stopped blessing and giving thanks for our food at meal times.

Coincidence? I think not. There's quite a bit of evidence suggesting a link.

The Power of Gratitude

Back in the 1850s and '60s, a clockmaker in Maine applied the scientific method to the idea of illness and found that there was a direct mental equivalent (thought, image, belief) for every physical ailment he experienced or encountered. He used this understanding to explain his own healing processes, then he began treating the mental state of people around him and found that their physical ailments would generally dissipate, and often disappear completely. Records indicate that close to 12,000 people were treated successfully in this way. His name was Phineas Parkhurst Quimby and he taught his Mental Healing method to several homeopathic physicians in his community, including one who came through town periodically, Dr. Mary Baker Patterson.

She later remarried and became Mary Baker Eddy, and used the methods she'd learned from Quimby to heal herself and teach people to become healers, and in time founded the Church of Christ, Scientist.

Others used his method, as well, but none taught as many practitioners as Mrs. Eddy—except one of her students, who developed her own understanding and went on to teach 11,000 people to heal themselves and teach others between 1886 and 1924. Her name was Emma Curtis Hopkins, and she's known as "the teacher of teachers" because her students included the founders of all the denominations of the New Thought movement: the Fillmores (Unity), Holmes (Science of Mind), Cramer & Brooks (Divine Science) and the Rix sisters (Homes of Truth). Louise Hay's *You Can Heal Your Life* is the simplest, most direct application of Quimby's method offered in print today.[48]

Theirs is the spiritual practice that enabled my own healing, years ago, and drew me into and became the focus of my ministry.

The essence of the practice, as Hopkins taught it, is to shift from thinking we are separated from our Good and begin to *feel* our Good, as G*d, present everywhere, in all things, and working in and through all experience. She taught that this constant, unending Grace is available to all, in all, and through all, if we allow it—and the most direct way to allow it is the overwhelming feeling of appreciation and gratitude for the good we are experiencing, now.

Once that fundamental shift in thinking is made, then we can leave behind all the contradictory thought patterns that have been learned and adopted over the course of a lifetime, and begin to replace them with new, truer ideas about ourselves, our lives, and our current state of well-being. Then we can begin to experience our natural interconnection with the energies of life, wisdom,

---

[48] For more details on the New Thought movement, explore these websites: www.unity.org; www.inta.org; www.csl.org. My book, *150 Years of Healing,* provides a brief overview of the teachers and their experiences. And my *Unveiling Your Hidden Power* provides a detailed introduction to Emma Hopkins' teachings.

harmony, and wellbeing. This is what Ralph Waldo Emerson called "Self-Reliance," in alignment with an always-supportive Nature.[49]

Many sacred texts are used to support and explain this way of being. They're drawn from every spiritual tradition on the planet, but perhaps because the U.S. is so deeply steeped in the Judeo-Christian tradition, many examples come from *Torah,* the prophets, the Psalms, and the New Testament.

One of those examples is the scene in the New Testament where Jesus (*Y'shua*, which means "Savior," "Salvation."), stands before a tomb and says "Father I thank you…" then commands "Lazarus, come forth!" and his dear friend Lazarus, who was buried 3 days before, comes out of the tomb. Another is the Hebrew story of the prophet Elijah (*Eliyahu*, which means "my God is YHVH") encouraging the woman who has nothing but a jar of oil to begin pouring that oil into as many jars as she can get her hands on as a demonstration of the unending supply that is available to us all.

In both stories, the expression of gratitude came before the experience! And, as New Thought teachers have discovered, it is always thus. We "ask, believing"—and therefore appreciating—in order to receive. We give thanks for the blessing in order to experience it. We express gratitude and appreciation for what we have in order to have more of it.

I'm fascinated that the word "appreciate" is used to describe an increase in value as well as to express our pleasure or enjoyment of something. When we appreciate something and act on that appreciation, it generally does increase in value. If we enjoy someone's work and let them know so, we're likely to get more of that level of work. When we pay someone well—perhaps even more than they asked or expect—we typically receive even better service the next time.

---

[49] My book, *Natural Abundance, Ralph Waldo Emerson's Guidelines for Prosperity,* is my "translation" of 5 of his most commonly known essays, with exercises, explaining his ideas.

What New Thought practitioners and teachers have found over the past 150 years is that whatever we focus our attention on increases, and what we express appreciation for is multiplied many times over.

And, as with everything else we've been saying in this book, this is not really a new idea: Not only was it expressed thousands of years ago in both the Christian and Jewish bibles, we know now that Indigenous peoples have maintained this awareness throughout the millennia. In the meantime Western culture, caught up in the linearity of the written word and the commitment to "progress" associated with that linearity, has lost it.

The Wise Ones in Indigenous cultures continue to bless and appreciate what they have, knowing that's the only way they and their people will continue to have it—or ever have more than what is visible in this moment. They know that gratitude and appreciation are the key to experiencing the grace of abundant Life.

We would all do well to remember it.

Speaking a Language of Life

"Organizations that are continually expanding their capacity to create their future require a fundamental shift of mind among their members." ~ *Peter Senge*[50]

Milt Markewitz

Prologue

In order for our culture to do the apparently impossible task of healing ourselves and our planet, I think we will need to mature so that we can shift our ways of thinking and acting. We need to bring to the surface some deeper, more integral ways of thinking, feeling, and being. Based on what I've seen I think these might include:

1) An appreciation of life;

2) An acceptance of Nature as a mentor and a model; and

3) A commitment to living in balance and harmony with the Earth.

These seem essential for any effective solution, but they're largely left out of Western culture processes.

If we look carefully at the A-I process, we see how critical consensus around both the 'Affirmative Topic of Choice' and the 'Positive Core' are to the success of the four phases. We can also see that in the Western approach to problem-solving the emphasis is on the former, while in the Indigenous and Eastern approaches the emphasis is on blending the two, with the 'Positive Core' deeply internalized by all parties.

Listening to Indigenous Voices

As part of my certification process in Appreciative Inquiry I was able to observe its use in other cultures and found that In-

---

[50] From the Learning Organization website: www.infed.org/thinkers/senge.htm

digenous peoples more readily operated out of deeply held ethics that were imbedded in their 'Positive Core'.

Looking at a sample of work from one indigenous leader, Chief Oren Lyons, the Faithkeeper of the Turtle Clan in the Onondaga Nation, helped me see the importance of the 'Positive Core' for three dilemmas, each with a different 'Affirmative Topic of Choice'.

My latest encounter with Chief Lyons was in October of 2011 at an American Indian Institute gathering. There he told us the story of the warring Iroquois tribes, and how they embarked on a 2-generation peace process that reconciled differences among the Iroquois tribes as well as with neighboring tribes. When the process was complete, the Elders who had led the process said that now it is time to learn how to govern ourselves—the time to learn democratic processes.

It's this work that informed the Founding Fathers who framed the U.S. Constitution with its governing system of checks and balances. Chief Lyons also shared with us the reservations these Elders had regarding what was to become the United States of America implementing the democracy they had envisioned. He said that they told our leaders that democracy would not work if there wasn't a healthy balance between men and women, that there was no place in a democracy for slavery, and that our concepts of property and ownership needed to change.

In the terminology of Appreciative Inquiry, we could say that the Founding Fathers were articulating this country's 'Positive Core' in the form of a Constitution, but the essence of that 'Core' was missing some critical elements, and it was doubtful that we could be successful without the learning and change that would lead us to include them.

Listening in Brazil

My first encounter with Chief Lyons was the video, *Yakoana*, which I described earlier in this book. It's a documentary of Indigenous Peoples from around the world who gathered for 10 days outside of Rio de Janeiro prior to the first UN Conference on Environment and Development in June of 1992. Chief Lyons was a participant at the conference, and spoke eloquently when interviewed. His was one of many stories documenting what has happened to indigenous peoples all over the world.

The stories are filled with anger and sadness at what is happening to our home, the Earth. And they are also filled with indigenous wisdom. Their collective story is captured on the video cover with the following quote:

> "...the stories, music, ceremony and dance of this historic gathering. *Yakoana* tells the story of the struggle of native cultures for recognition and human rights, as well as their ancient ways of living sustainably and in harmony with the earth. It presents the indigenous peoples' world view, which sees humanity as part of the sacred web of nature." ~ Anh Crutcher Oppenheimer [51]

The point of the 10-day gathering was to develop relationships for the first several days, and then develop a mutually agreed statement for their spokesperson, Marcus Terena, to present in the 5 minutes allocated on the agenda for the Indigenous voice.

Throughout Terena's speech at the conference, and all the stories that were shared prior to the conference, there was a visible dignity—not only in how individuals representing their tribes, but in how they appealed to the best from those cultures who bore responsibility for the atrocities and current calamities. The guiding principles they shared, their 'Positive Core', was rock solid and provided an ethical compass that never wavered. It is what appears to be their salvation in both overcoming the atrocities of colonialism and leading a sustainability movement for the world that makes sense.

Listening in Australia

My second encounter with Chief Lyons was at the Parliament of World Religions in Melbourne, Australia in December of 2009. He was the first of four panelists addressing the question,

---

[51] dvd jacket, *Yakoana the Voice of Indigenous Peoples,* produced and directed by Anh Crutcher Oppenheimer and Edited by Vivien Hillgrove.

"What is the Religious Response to the Crisis of our Time, Global Climate Change?"

He explained the relationship of the Native Americans to the Earth and the importance of living every act of life in harmony with the natural world. He also spoke of his people prophesying this crisis when they observed how the norms of Western cultures were out of balance and harmony as evidenced by our disrespect for life. When the session was over, I introduced myself to Chief Lyons and told him that although I wasn't Native American, I had a deep listening and resonance with what he'd said. I also mentioned my impression that as each of the next three speakers spoke, they seemed to move progressively away from the Indigenous perspective as they focused on technical and political problems and solutions rather than accept responsibility and address the lifestyle changes necessary to achieve right relationship with the natural world. He responded by smiling and saying that he's been listening for years and the understanding hadn't been forthcoming.

Next I introduced myself to Mary Evelyn Tucker, a Senior Lecturer and Scholar in the Yale University departments of Environmental Studies, Divinity, and Religious Studies, who facilitated the panel. I told her how much I appreciated her work with Father Thomas Berry, and that I thought the 'Religious Response' might better develop from his work. She said that there would be a 'Thomas Berry' session the next day, and encouraged me to attend.

I attended and I wasn't disappointed. Thomas Berry's protégées shared his book, *The Work of Our Time*, and one in particular, a Canadian professor named Anne Marie Dalton, captured for me the shift of mind, heart, and spirit needed to discern life with all its beauty and sensuality; with awe and reverence; and with a sense of appreciation that extends to all life and to future generations. This session paralleled Chief Lyons' opening of the previous session regarding the need to shift our attention from the economic to the ecological; to rethink our concepts of property and ownership; to reflect on our deepest 'truths' regarding the dualities imbedded in many of our religious and spiritual beliefs; and to be sure that these values are shared by our political representatives at all levels.

I was very heartened by this work, particularly when I learned that members of the Obama administration were attending the Parliament of World Religions and it seemed that both Mary Evelyn and Chief Lyons had their ear.

While in Australia in 2009, I also had the pleasure of listening to a young Aboriginal elder who shared with us his nomadic existence, and how his knowing and being are incorporated in his people's Dreamtime. This ancient, continually unfolding story is all that is necessary to see abundance where most of us would see barren wilderness; to live harmoniously with Nature; and to be a functional part of community.

All of this seems to stem from their cosmology, their understanding of how the land and life forms were (and are) created, and their sense of purpose in the Universe. This young Elder introduced himself as illiterate—dyslexic—and now he is just learning to read and write. But his wisdom went far beyond any learning he will ever get from books. He was, in Western terminology, a shaman or mystic.

He explained the Dreamtime in terms of an annual trek in which time was measured by the growing seasons (that changed each year due to weather conditions) of six food sources. The Dreamtime walk was all part of an incredible sense of place–for sustenance, life passage events, ceremonies, and even for dying. It's part of their connection with ancestors and future generations. In his description, there was an energetic connection with the Earth that was described in terms of vortexes like knowing where water ran underground by sensing the energy.

He had time for a few questions, and the overwhelming sentiment was a deep resonance, along with the question, "Where had this person been, and why hadn't his story been told before?" His response was also filled with surprise, and perhaps a hint of anger, "Why haven't you been listening?"

The session closing was an invitation to participate in an Aboriginal dance, and when our shaman leader danced you could feel his connection to the animals that essentially choreographed his steps and motions.

Listening Between Agencies

In the Portland area there are many examples of Native American organizations that seem to me to be grounded in what I've begun to call an 'Indigenous-oriented Positive Core'. Their focus is primarily on restoring wholeness to tribal people who suffer the affects of colonization and urbanization: addictions, poverty, suicides, and mental health issues.

They've found that Western approaches for addressing these problems often exacerbate them, so the focus of the Native organizations is on bringing these people into community and ceremony. Thus they can be true to the guiding principles of their 'Positive Core'.

Some organizations are also focused on sustainability, and there is much to be learned from the 'Renewable Energy Feasibility Study' developed by the Confederated Tribes of the Umatilla Indian reservation, the work of the Columbia River Inter-Tribal Fisheries Commission, the Indigenous Education Institute, and many other tribes and confederations throughout the US, Canada, and Alaska.

In October of 2112, at the North American Association of Environmental Educators, I heard another example of listening that I believe is worth sharing. It regards a collaborative effort among the US Forest Service Pacific Southwest Research Station, Prescott College, and the North Fork Mono Native American nation, focused on saving a local watershed. When the native speaker, Mr. Ron Goode, spoke, he told his Native Creation Story, and the wisdom of how water rises in the land was embedded in that story As I remember the session, the approaches suggested by the non-native attendees included digging to create a lake. The Native American approach, to allow water to rise in seven meadows of the watershed, was the one selected. It was the first time I've heard of Native wisdom prevailing over a Western proposed solution, and I remain deeply heartened.

Living Language, Sustainable Life

"...it is necessary to look backward in order to go forward – to draw on the wisdom of the true "(ab)original thought" that transcends time. So while Western science considers the notion of non-locality to be an exciting frontier to investigate, this realm is a given in Native science. To Native people, thought, or spirit is and always has been alive and moving." ~ *Glenn Aparicio Parry* [52]

Milt Markewitz & Ruth L. Miller

While the world's issues have reached crisis proportions on all fronts, what we need to do is clear—and that alone inspires hope.

First, we know what transformation is needed—an ethic of living in balance and harmony with the Earth—and that this key, essential transformation isn't new. Instead of a difficult linear leap forward to a place humanity has never been, we can make a circular change to a tried-and-true method, choosing ways that have been lived for millennia and are still being lived by some today. The knowledge, wisdom, leadership, language, and examples are all available: we can all practice Sacred Ecology.

Second, we can now look at our language and culture as being less enlightened than we might once have thought and we can learn for ourselves, and encourage our children to learn, an ancient language. Doing so will modify our culture's thinking to be more in relationship with all life, and so better understand what brings each of us personal vitality, health, and happiness, as well as communal well-being.

Third, we can recognize something that Marcus Terena said in his speech to the first UN Conference on Environment and Development in Rio de Janeiro in June of 1992,

> This life code that no scientist has ever managed to unveil rests with the Indians. You don't have to look any further. Are

---

[52] Glenn Aparicio Parry, IONS Journal #9, page 30

you prepared for that? Is the contemporary world prepared for what we want to convey after 500 years of silence?

Could Terena's "life code" be akin to the Qabala? Could the ancient wisdom entrusted to Moses be the same wisdom held by Indigenous peoples today? It's worth exploring—for all our well-being.

Fourth, once the listening happens, people all over the world are taking action—and we can, too. Paul Hawken's *Blessed Unrest*[53] documents millions of non-profits, many of which are focused on the environment, in which people are doing their 'life-work' of restoring well-being to humanity and the planet. Other examples of this kind of listening abound.

Finding Answers

Perhaps all the answers we seek are embedded in the wisdom of Indigenous peoples—a wisdom that is understood by whole cultures because it's part of the language they speak, and it's internalized as they combine thinking in multiple generations with attempting to live each day according to the ethical code inherent in their language.

Ancient spoken Hebrew appears to have been one of those languages, and discerning the ancient Hebrew through the lens provided by Carlos Suares gives us great insights. First it shows us the three worlds in which we exist, each with an apparently different science, and it shows us the potential interplay among these worlds in our evolving experience. Perhaps more importantly, the 9 columns in his matrix of the Hebrew characters inform us about the necessary and sufficient processes for all life to flourish—processes that Western science, through Living Systems Theory, is just beginning to comprehend.

Indigenous people know, and Westerners are beginning to understand, that we are all part of a set of life processes, a life-death-life continuum, embedded in perfect order, with the capacity to perpetuate life with both uniqueness and integrity, and

---

[53] Found at http://www.blessedunrest.com/.

attracted physically and emotionally to all that we need as part of the universal dance of life.

When we all fully understand this, when it is part of our Positive Core, then possibilities for a new destiny abound. And when we experience it daily, through our language and spiritual practice, our individual lives become contributions to the harmonious and sustainable processes of planetary and universal Life.

...And so we come to a completion—and, as always must be in every ending, a beginning. Let us now, as we did at the end of the Binding of Isaac story which launched this whole process, say this vibrant set of shamanic characters:

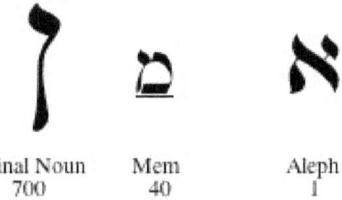

Final Noun 700   Mem 40   Aleph 1

With all the infinite possibilities and combinations of what might be, the final *Noun* creates a beautiful Life-Death-Life Continuum, as we say...

Aleph—we give thanks for this moment and commit ourselves to what has been birthed—*Mem... Amen.*

Gratitudes

By Milt—

This whole book is grounded in appreciation for life, and much of that appreciation is for friends and family who offered inspiration and direct support.

Ms. Joanie Levine who out of the blue offered to edit the chapters I'd drafted, and added much value to the book.

Ms. Batya Podos, my story-telling mentor and friend, who help shape my understanding of both the first day of creation and how Moses' father-in-law and Priest of the Midian, Yitro, may have advised him very differently than what is normally understood from most Torah readings.

All the colleagues and mentors whose voices resonated so deeply.

My mother who challenged me to listen and learn.

My father whose voice it is I hear when listening to the Indigenous elders.

By Ruth—

Milt's willingness to trust me with his ideas, even to expand on them, is deeply appreciated. I hope I've been helpful.

My deep gratitude also to all the professors and colleagues—in cultural theory, linguistics, and systems thinking—who helped me to see the world and humanity as a holon, with language as a major determiner of our experience—including the late Steven D. Rogers, a great promoter of systemic thought, who helped form and maintain the Cascades Systems Society, where Milt and I and others have explored these kinds of ideas.

And, for clarity about the Trikaya model, all thanks to Robert Bruce Newman, meditation master and lead co-author of our book, Empowered Care: Mind-Body Medicine Methods.

Other Titles from Portal Center Press

Kat's 9 Lives, moving passion into action for a "feel good" life, by Kat Cunningham

Kindred Spirits: the quest for love and friendship, by Bob Czimbal & Maggie Zadikov

Make the World Go Away, the gift of 2012, by Ruth L. Miller

Mary's Power, Embracing the Divine Feminine as the Age of Invasion and Empire Ends, by Ruth L Miller

Views from the Pew, moving beyond religion – discovering truth within, by J C Pedigo and friends

Wake UP! Our old beliefs don't work anymore! by Andree L. Cuenod

www.portalcenterpress.com • 541-351-8461